# TEACHER'S PET PUBLICATIONS

## PUZZLE PACK
for
Dr. Jekyll and Mr. Hyde

based on the book by
Robert Louis Stevenson

Written by
William T. Collins

© 2005 Teacher's Pet Publications
All Rights Reserved

The materials in this packet are copyrighted
by Teacher's Pet Publications, Inc.

These pages may be duplicated by the purchaser
for use in the purchaser's own classroom.

Copying any of these materials and distributing them
for any other purpose is a violation of the copyright laws.

© 2005 Teacher's Pet Publications, Inc.
www.tpet.com

## INTRODUCTION
If you already own the LitPlan for this title, this Puzzle Pack will refresh your Unit Resource Materials and Vocabulary Resource Materials sections plus give you additional materials you can substitute into the tests. If you do not already have a complete LitPlan, these pages will give you some supplemental materials to use with your own plan. There are two main groups of materials: one set for unit words (such as characters' names, symbols, places, etc.) and one set for vocabulary words associated with the book.

## WORD LIST
There is a word list for both the unit words and the vocabulary words. These lists show you which words are being used in the materials and the clues or definitions being used for those words. You may want to give students a word list with clues/definitions to help them, or you may want students to only have a word list (without clues/definitions) if you want them to work a little harder. Both are available for duplication. The word lists can also be your "calling key" for the bingo games.

## FILL IN THE BLANK AND MATCHING
There are 4 each of the fill in the blank and matching worksheets for both the unit and vocabulary words. These pages can be used either as extra worksheets for students or as objective parts of a unit test. They can be done individually if students need extra help or as a whole class activity to review the material covered.

## MAGIC SQUARES
The magic squares not only reinforce the material covered but also work on reasoning and math skills. Many teachers have told us that their students really enjoy doing these!

## WORD SEARCH PUZZLES
The word search words go in all directions, as indicated on your answer keys. Two of the word search puzzles have the clues listed rather than the words. This makes the puzzle a little more difficult, but it reinforces the material better. Two word search puzzles have words only for students who find the clue puzzles too difficult.

## CROSSWORD PUZZLES
Both unit and vocabulary word sections have 4 crossword puzzles.

## BINGO CARDS
There are 32 individual bingo cards for the unit words and 32 individual bingo cards for the vocabulary words. You can use your word list as a "call list," calling the words at random and marking them off of your list as you go, or you could use the flash cards by cutting them apart and drawing the words at random from a hat (or box or whatever). To make a better review, you might ask for the definition and spelling of each word as you call it out–or you could call out the definitions and have students tell you the words they need to look for on the puzzle.

## JUGGLE LETTERS
The vocabulary juggle letter game is intended to help students learn the spellings of the words. One sheet has the definitions listed on it as an extra help for students who need it or to reinforce the definitions if you choose to do so.

## FLASH CARDS
We've included a set of vocabulary flash cards you can duplicate, cut, and fold for your students. Some teachers make a few sets for general use by the class; others make a set for each student. Some teachers duplicate them for each student and have the students cut & fold their own. You can cut out just the words and put them in a hat, have each student pick out one word and write the definition and a sentence for that word. Students then swap words and papers, with the next student adding a sentence of his own under the last one. You can have students swap as many times as you like. Each time the student will read the sentences written prior to his own and then add a sentence. You can cut out the words and definitions separately and play "I Have; Who Has?" Each student in the room draws a word and definition. The first student says, "I have (the name of the word). Who has the definition?" The student with the definition reads it then says, "I have (the name of the vocabulary word she has). Who has the definition?" The round continues until all words and definitions have been given.

## Dr. Jekyll & Mr. Hyde Word List

| No. | Word | Clue/Definition |
|---|---|---|
| 1. | BLACK MAIL | ____House: Mr. Enfield's name for the residence |
| 2. | BRADSHAW | Footman |
| 3. | CANE | Murder weapon |
| 4. | CAVENDISH | ____Square: location of Dr. Lanyon's home |
| 5. | CHEQUE BOOK | Mr. Utterson took it from the fire |
| 6. | DANVERS | First name of murdered man |
| 7. | DENMAN | Surgical theater |
| 8. | DRAWER | Dr. Lanyon held it for Dr. Jekyll |
| 9. | DRUGS | Caused the change from Jekyll to Hyde |
| 10. | EDINBURGH | Dr. Jekyll's accent |
| 11. | EDWARD | Mr. Hyde's first name |
| 12. | EIGHT | ____or ten: trampled girl's age |
| 13. | ENFIELD | Saw Mr. Hyde trample a girl |
| 14. | GABRIEL | Mr. Utterson's first name |
| 15. | GAIETY | Dr. Jekyll didn't like it about himself |
| 16. | GALLOWS | Hyde feared this |
| 17. | GREEN | Third color of the liquid/cheque book color |
| 18. | GUEST | Identified similarity in writings |
| 19. | HARRY | Dr. Jekyll's nickname |
| 20. | HASTIE | Dr. Lanyon's first name |
| 21. | HATRED | Dr. Jekyll and Mr. Hyde felt this for each other |
| 22. | HENRY | Dr. Jekyll's first name |
| 23. | HOUSEKEEPER | Was glad Mr. Hyde was in trouble |
| 24. | HYDE | Pure evil |
| 25. | JANUARY | Mr. Utterson dined at Dr. Jekyll's in this month |
| 26. | JEKYLL | Combination of good and evil |
| 27. | JOHN | Mr. Utterson's middle name |
| 28. | LANYON | Disagreed with Dr. Jekyll's methods |
| 29. | LONDON | Setting of novel |
| 30. | MAID | Witnessed the murder |
| 31. | MAW | Messrs.____:wholesale chemists |
| 32. | MIDNIGHT | Time of murder/time the messenger came |
| 33. | NEWCOMEN | Inspector |
| 34. | NINETY | Pounds for which the cheque was written |
| 35. | NINTH | Dr. Lanyon received the letter on this date |
| 36. | ONE HUNDRED | Pounds Mr. Hyde gave the family |
| 37. | PARLIAMENT | Sir Danvers Carew was a member of ____. |
| 38. | POOLE | Dr. Jekyll's servant |
| 39. | PORTLAND | ____ Street: Mr. Hyde drove to a hotel there |
| 40. | PURPLE | Second color of the liquid |
| 41. | RED | First color of the liquid |
| 42. | REGENT'S | ____Park: Dr. Jekyll involuntarily changed to Mr. Hyde here |
| 43. | RICHARD | Mr. Enfield's first name |
| 44. | SCOTLAND | The Inspector worked at____Yard |
| 45. | SIX | Hours Dr. Jekyll could go before changing to Mr. Hyde |
| 46. | SOHO | Location of Mr. Hyde's house |
| 47. | SUNDAY | Mr. Utterson and Mr. Enfield's walking day |
| 48. | TEN | # of years Dr. Lanyon had not seen Dr. Jekyll |
| 49. | TERROR | Dr. Lanyon felt this after his discovery |
| 50. | THREE | AM time when girl was trampled |
| 51. | UTTERSON | Dr. Jekyll's lawyer |
| 52. | WALKS | Mr. Utterson and Mr. Enfield took them |
| 53. | WILL | Mr. Utterson had Dr. Jekyll's |

# Dr. Jekyll & Mr. Hyde Fill In The Blank 1

_____  1. Dr. Jekyll's nickname

_____  2. ____ or ten: trampled girl's age

_____  3. Pounds Mr. Hyde gave the family

_____  4. Setting of novel

_____  5. Mr. Utterson had Dr. Jekyll's

_____  6. AM time when girl was trampled

_____  7. Mr. Utterson's middle name

_____  8. Dr. Jekyll's lawyer

_____  9. Identified similarity in writings

_____  10. Time of murder/time the messenger came

_____  11. The Inspector worked at ____ Yard

_____  12. Second color of the liquid

_____  13. Pure evil

_____  14. Mr. Utterson dined at Dr. Jekyll's in this month

_____  15. ____ House: Mr. Enfield's name for the residence

_____  16. Dr. Jekyll's accent

_____  17. Hours Dr. Jekyll could go before changing to Mr. Hyde

_____  18. Messrs. ____ : wholesale chemists

_____  19. Dr. Jekyll's first name

_____  20. Pounds for which the cheque was written

Dr. Jekyll & Mr. Hyde Fill In The Blank 1 Answer Key

|  |  |
|---|---|
| HARRY | 1. Dr. Jekyll's nickname |
| EIGHT | 2. ____ or ten: trampled girl's age |
| ONE HUNDRED | 3. Pounds Mr. Hyde gave the family |
| LONDON | 4. Setting of novel |
| WILL | 5. Mr. Utterson had Dr. Jekyll's |
| THREE | 6. AM time when girl was trampled |
| JOHN | 7. Mr. Utterson's middle name |
| UTTERSON | 8. Dr. Jekyll's lawyer |
| GUEST | 9. Identified similarity in writings |
| MIDNIGHT | 10. Time of murder/time the messenger came |
| SCOTLAND | 11. The Inspector worked at ____ Yard |
| PURPLE | 12. Second color of the liquid |
| HYDE | 13. Pure evil |
| JANUARY | 14. Mr. Utterson dined at Dr. Jekyll's in this month |
| BLACK MAIL | 15. ____ House: Mr. Enfield's name for the residence |
| EDINBURGH | 16. Dr. Jekyll's accent |
| SIX | 17. Hours Dr. Jekyll could go before changing to Mr. Hyde |
| MAW | 18. Messrs. ____ :wholesale chemists |
| HENRY | 19. Dr. Jekyll's first name |
| NINETY | 20. Pounds for which the cheque was written |

# Dr. Jekyll & Mr. Hyde Fill In The Blank 2

_____  1. Dr. Jekyll's lawyer

_____  2. Mr. Utterson and Mr. Enfield took them

_____  3. Surgical theater

_____  4. Mr. Hyde's first name

_____  5. Footman

_____  6. Sir Danvers Carew was a member of _____.

_____  7. First color of the liquid

_____  8. Dr. Lanyon's first name

_____  9. Witnessed the murder

_____  10. Mr. Utterson took it from the fire

_____  11. Dr. Lanyon received the letter on this date

_____  12. Mr. Utterson dined at Dr. Jekyll's in this month

_____  13. Dr. Jekyll and Mr. Hyde felt this for each other

_____  14. # of years Dr. Lanyon had not seen Dr. Jekyll

_____  15. ____Square: location of Dr. Lanyon's home

_____  16. Murder weapon

_____  17. Third color of the liquid/cheque book color

_____  18. Pounds Mr. Hyde gave the family

_____  19. Pure evil

_____  20. Dr. Lanyon felt this after his discovery

Dr. Jekyll & Mr. Hyde Fill In The Blank 2 Answer Key

|  |  |
|---|---|
| UTTERSON | 1. Dr. Jekyll's lawyer |
| WALKS | 2. Mr. Utterson and Mr. Enfield took them |
| DENMAN | 3. Surgical theater |
| EDWARD | 4. Mr. Hyde's first name |
| BRADSHAW | 5. Footman |
| PARLIAMENT | 6. Sir Danvers Carew was a member of _____. |
| RED | 7. First color of the liquid |
| HASTIE | 8. Dr. Lanyon's first name |
| MAID | 9. Witnessed the murder |
| CHEQUE BOOK | 10. Mr. Utterson took it from the fire |
| NINTH | 11. Dr. Lanyon received the letter on this date |
| JANUARY | 12. Mr. Utterson dined at Dr. Jekyll's in this month |
| HATRED | 13. Dr. Jekyll and Mr. Hyde felt this for each other |
| TEN | 14. # of years Dr. Lanyon had not seen Dr. Jekyll |
| CAVENDISH | 15. ____Square: location of Dr. Lanyon's home |
| CANE | 16. Murder weapon |
| GREEN | 17. Third color of the liquid/cheque book color |
| ONE HUNDRED | 18. Pounds Mr. Hyde gave the family |
| HYDE | 19. Pure evil |
| TERROR | 20. Dr. Lanyon felt this after his discovery |

Dr. Jekyll & Mr. Hyde Fill In The Blank 3

_____ 1. Murder weapon

_____ 2. Was glad Mr. Hyde was in trouble

_____ 3. Pounds Mr. Hyde gave the family

_____ 4. Inspector

_____ 5. Hyde feared this

_____ 6. Dr. Lanyon's first name

_____ 7. Mr. Utterson's middle name

_____ 8. Caused the change from Jekyll to Hyde

_____ 9. Dr. Jekyll's accent

_____ 10. Dr. Lanyon received the letter on this date

_____ 11. Surgical theater

_____ 12. Mr. Utterson took it from the fire

_____ 13. Mr. Utterson had Dr. Jekyll's

_____ 14. Third color of the liquid/cheque book color

_____ 15. Combination of good and evil

_____ 16. Sir Danvers Carew was a member of _____.

_____ 17. Mr. Utterson dined at Dr. Jekyll's in this month

_____ 18. ____ Street: Mr. Hyde drove to a hotel there

_____ 19. Saw Mr. Hyde trample a girl

_____ 20. Second color of the liquid

Dr. Jekyll & Mr. Hyde Fill In The Blank 3 Answer Key

| | |
|---|---|
| CANE | 1. Murder weapon |
| HOUSEKEEPER | 2. Was glad Mr. Hyde was in trouble |
| ONE HUNDRED | 3. Pounds Mr. Hyde gave the family |
| NEWCOMEN | 4. Inspector |
| GALLOWS | 5. Hyde feared this |
| HASTIE | 6. Dr. Lanyon's first name |
| JOHN | 7. Mr. Utterson's middle name |
| DRUGS | 8. Caused the change from Jekyll to Hyde |
| EDINBURGH | 9. Dr. Jekyll's accent |
| NINTH | 10. Dr. Lanyon received the letter on this date |
| DENMAN | 11. Surgical theater |
| CHEQUE BOOK | 12. Mr. Utterson took it from the fire |
| WILL | 13. Mr. Utterson had Dr. Jekyll's |
| GREEN | 14. Third color of the liquid/cheque book color |
| JEKYLL | 15. Combination of good and evil |
| PARLIAMENT | 16. Sir Danvers Carew was a member of _____. |
| JANUARY | 17. Mr. Utterson dined at Dr. Jekyll's in this month |
| PORTLAND | 18. ____ Street: Mr. Hyde drove to a hotel there |
| ENFIELD | 19. Saw Mr. Hyde trample a girl |
| PURPLE | 20. Second color of the liquid |

Dr. Jekyll & Mr. Hyde Fill In The Blank 4

_____  1. Mr. Utterson and Mr. Enfield took them

_____  2. Second color of the liquid

_____  3. Hours Dr. Jekyll could go before changing to Mr. Hyde

_____  4. Dr. Jekyll's accent

_____  5. Sir Danvers Carew was a member of _____.

_____  6. Mr. Utterson took it from the fire

_____  7. Dr. Jekyll's nickname

_____  8. Mr. Utterson's first name

_____  9. Surgical theater

_____ 10. ____Park: Dr. Jekyll involuntarily changed to Mr. Hyde here

_____ 11. Mr. Utterson's middle name

_____ 12. ____ Street: Mr. Hyde drove to a hotel there

_____ 13. Dr. Jekyll's servant

_____ 14. Mr. Hyde's first name

_____ 15. Dr. Jekyll didn't like it about himself

_____ 16. Dr. Lanyon received the letter on this date

_____ 17. Ttime of murder/time the messenger came

_____ 18. Mr. Utterson dined at Dr. Jekyll's in this month

_____ 19. Mr. Utterson and Mr. Enfield's walking day

_____ 20. Footman

Dr. Jekyll & Mr. Hyde Fill In The Blank 4 Answer Key

| | |
|---|---|
| WALKS | 1. Mr. Utterson and Mr. Enfield took them |
| PURPLE | 2. Second color of the liquid |
| SIX | 3. Hours Dr. Jekyll could go before changing to Mr. Hyde |
| EDINBURGH | 4. Dr. Jekyll's accent |
| PARLIAMENT | 5. Sir Danvers Carew was a member of _____. |
| CHEQUE BOOK | 6. Mr. Utterson took it from the fire |
| HARRY | 7. Dr. Jekyll's nickname |
| GABRIEL | 8. Mr. Utterson's first name |
| DENMAN | 9. Surgical theater |
| REGENT'S | 10. ____Park: Dr. Jekyll involuntarily changed to Mr. Hyde here |
| JOHN | 11. Mr. Utterson's middle name |
| PORTLAND | 12. ____ Street: Mr. Hyde drove to a hotel there |
| POOLE | 13. Dr. Jekyll's servant |
| EDWARD | 14. Mr. Hyde's first name |
| GAIETY | 15. Dr. Jekyll didn't like it about himself |
| NINTH | 16. Dr. Lanyon received the letter on this date |
| MIDNIGHT | 17. Time of murder/time the messenger came |
| JANUARY | 18. Mr. Utterson dined at Dr. Jekyll's in this month |
| SUNDAY | 19. Mr. Utterson and Mr. Enfield's walking day |
| BRADSHAW | 20. Footman |

Dr. Jekyll & Mr. Hyde Matching 1

___ 1. HATRED           A. Dr. Jekyll didn't like it about himself
___ 2. TEN              B. Disagreed with Dr. Jekyll's methods
___ 3. ENFIELD          C. Caused the change from Jekyll to Hyde
___ 4. DRUGS            D. Mr. Utterson had Dr. Jekyll's
___ 5. EDWARD           E. ____Square: location of Dr. Lanyon's home
___ 6. GAIETY           F. Mr. Utterson's first name
___ 7. MAID             G. # of years Dr. Lanyon had not seen Dr. Jekyll
___ 8. SOHO             H. Dr. Jekyll and Mr. Hyde felt this for each other
___ 9. WILL             I. ____House: Mr. Enfield's name for the residence
___10. UTTERSON         J. Witnessed the murder
___11. JOHN             K. Murder weapon
___12. BRADSHAW         L. Saw Mr. Hyde trample a girl
___13. GABRIEL          M. Hours Dr. Jekyll could go before changing to Mr. Hyde
___14. EDINBURGH        N. Dr. Jekyll's lawyer
___15. HYDE             O. Pure evil
___16. DENMAN           P. Pounds Mr. Hyde gave the family
___17. POOLE            Q. Dr. Jekyll's accent
___18. SIX              R. Surgical theater
___19. BLACK MAIL       S. Location of Mr. Hyde's house
___20. NEWCOMEN         T. Footman
___21. CANE             U. Mr. Utterson's middle name
___22. LANYON           V. Inspector
___23. ONE HUNDRED      W. Mr. Hyde's first name
___24. THREE            X. AM time when girl was trampled
___25. CAVENDISH        Y. Dr. Jekyll's servant

Dr. Jekyll & Mr. Hyde Matching 1 Answer Key

| | | |
|---|---|---|
| H - 1. HATRED | A. | Dr. Jekyll didn't like it about himself |
| G - 2. TEN | B. | Disagreed with Dr. Jekyll's methods |
| L - 3. ENFIELD | C. | Caused the change from Jekyll to Hyde |
| C - 4. DRUGS | D. | Mr. Utterson had Dr. Jekyll's |
| W - 5. EDWARD | E. | ____Square: location of Dr. Lanyon's home |
| A - 6. GAIETY | F. | Mr. Utterson's first name |
| J - 7. MAID | G. | # of years Dr. Lanyon had not seen Dr. Jekyll |
| S - 8. SOHO | H. | Dr. Jekyll and Mr. Hyde felt this for each other |
| D - 9. WILL | I. | ____House: Mr. Enfield's name for the residence |
| N - 10. UTTERSON | J. | Witnessed the murder |
| U - 11. JOHN | K. | Murder weapon |
| T - 12. BRADSHAW | L. | Saw Mr. Hyde trample a girl |
| F - 13. GABRIEL | M. | Hours Dr. Jekyll could go before changing to Mr. Hyde |
| Q - 14. EDINBURGH | N. | Dr. Jekyll's lawyer |
| O - 15. HYDE | O. | Pure evil |
| R - 16. DENMAN | P. | Pounds Mr. Hyde gave the family |
| Y - 17. POOLE | Q. | Dr. Jekyll's accent |
| M - 18. SIX | R. | Surgical theater |
| I - 19. BLACK MAIL | S. | Location of Mr. Hyde's house |
| V - 20. NEWCOMEN | T. | Footman |
| K - 21. CANE | U. | Mr. Utterson's middle name |
| B - 22. LANYON | V. | Inspector |
| P - 23. ONE HUNDRED | W. | Mr. Hyde's first name |
| X - 24. THREE | X. | AM time when girl was trampled |
| E - 25. CAVENDISH | Y. | Dr. Jekyll's servant |

Dr. Jekyll & Mr. Hyde Matching 2

___ 1. GAIETY
___ 2. REGENT'S
___ 3. DENMAN
___ 4. HARRY
___ 5. HASTIE
___ 6. DRAWER
___ 7. TERROR
___ 8. SUNDAY
___ 9. EIGHT
___ 10. GALLOWS
___ 11. EDWARD
___ 12. MAID
___ 13. POOLE
___ 14. NINETY
___ 15. PORTLAND
___ 16. UTTERSON
___ 17. CAVENDISH
___ 18. LANYON
___ 19. ONE HUNDRED
___ 20. WILL
___ 21. PARLIAMENT
___ 22. GABRIEL
___ 23. BLACK MAIL
___ 24. NINTH
___ 25. HENRY

A. ____ or ten: trampled girl's age
B. Mr. Hyde's first name
C. ____ Park: Dr. Jekyll involuntarily changed to Mr. Hyde here
D. Disagreed with Dr. Jekyll's methods
E. Mr. Utterson had Dr. Jekyll's
F. Dr. Jekyll's first name
G. Dr. Jekyll's servant
H. Sir Danvers Carew was a member of _____.
I. ____ Square: location of Dr. Lanyon's home
J. Dr. Jekyll's lawyer
K. Dr. Jekyll's nickname
L. Dr. Lanyon held for Dr. Jekyll
M. Pounds Mr. Hyde gave the family
N. Surgical theater
O. Mr. Utterson's first name
P. ____ Street: Mr. Hyde drove to a hotel there
Q. ____ House: Mr. Enfield's name for the residence
R. Hyde feared this
S. Dr. Lanyon felt this after his discovery
T. Dr. Lanyon received the letter on this date
U. Witnessed the murder
V. Dr. Jekyll didn't like it about himself
W. Pounds for which the cheque was written
X. Dr. Lanyon's first name
Y. Mr. Utterson and Mr. Enfield's walking day

# Dr. Jekyll & Mr. Hyde Matching 2 Answer Key

| | | |
|---|---|---|
| V - 1. GAIETY | A. | ____ or ten: trampled girl's age |
| C - 2. REGENT'S | B. | Mr. Hyde's first name |
| N - 3. DENMAN | C. | ____ Park: Dr. Jekyll involuntarily changed to Mr. Hyde here |
| K - 4. HARRY | D. | Disagreed with Dr. Jekyll's methods |
| X - 5. HASTIE | E. | Mr. Utterson had Dr. Jekyll's |
| L - 6. DRAWER | F. | Dr. Jekyll's first name |
| S - 7. TERROR | G. | Dr. Jekyll's servant |
| Y - 8. SUNDAY | H. | Sir Danvers Carew was a member of _____. |
| A - 9. EIGHT | I. | ____ Square: location of Dr. Lanyon's home |
| R -10. GALLOWS | J. | Dr. Jekyll's lawyer |
| B -11. EDWARD | K. | Dr. Jekyll's nickname |
| U -12. MAID | L. | Dr. Lanyon held it for Dr. Jekyll |
| G -13. POOLE | M. | Pounds Mr. Hyde gave the family |
| W -14. NINETY | N. | Surgical theater |
| P -15. PORTLAND | O. | Mr. Utterson's first name |
| J -16. UTTERSON | P. | ____ Street: Mr. Hyde drove to a hotel there |
| I -17. CAVENDISH | Q. | ____ House: Mr. Enfield's name for the residence |
| D -18. LANYON | R. | Hyde feared this |
| M -19. ONE HUNDRED | S. | Dr. Lanyon felt this after his discovery |
| E -20. WILL | T. | Dr. Lanyon received the letter on this date |
| H -21. PARLIAMENT | U. | Witnessed the murder |
| O -22. GABRIEL | V. | Dr. Jekyll didn't like it about himself |
| Q -23. BLACK MAIL | W. | Pounds for which the cheque was written |
| T -24. NINTH | X. | Dr. Lanyon's first name |
| F -25. HENRY | Y. | Mr. Utterson and Mr. Enfield's walking day |

Dr. Jekyll & Mr. Hyde Matching 3

___ 1. MIDNIGHT
___ 2. PARLIAMENT
___ 3. GALLOWS
___ 4. JEKYLL
___ 5. EIGHT
___ 6. DENMAN
___ 7. SIX
___ 8. JOHN
___ 9. GABRIEL
___ 10. BRADSHAW
___ 11. EDWARD
___ 12. RICHARD
___ 13. HASTIE
___ 14. CAVENDISH
___ 15. MAID
___ 16. UTTERSON
___ 17. LONDON
___ 18. NEWCOMEN
___ 19. LANYON
___ 20. NINTH
___ 21. TEN
___ 22. DRAWER
___ 23. ONE HUNDRED
___ 24. MAW
___ 25. TERROR

A. Dr. Lanyon's first name
B. Messrs.____:wholesale chemists
C. Setting of novel
D. Sir Danvers Carew was a member of _____.
E. ____Square: location of Dr. Lanyon's home
F. Footman
G. Pounds Mr. Hyde gave the family
H. Witnessed the murder
I. ____or ten: trampled girl's age
J. Disagreed with Dr. Jekyll's methods
K. Inspector
L. Time of murder/time the messenger came
M. Mr. Hyde's first name
N. Combination of good and evil
O. Surgical theater
P. Dr. Jekyll's lawyer
Q. Hyde feared this
R. Mr. Utterson's first name
S. Hours Dr. Jekyll could go before changing to Mr. Hyde
T. Dr. Lanyon held it for Dr. Jekyll
U. Mr. Enfield's first name
V. Dr. Lanyon felt this after his discovery
W. Mr. Utterson's middle name
X. # of years Dr. Lanyon had not seen Dr. Jekyll
Y. Dr. Lanyon received the letter on this date

Dr. Jekyll & Mr. Hyde Matching 3 Answer Key

| | | |
|---|---|---|
| L - 1. MIDNIGHT | A. | Dr. Lanyon's first name |
| D - 2. PARLIAMENT | B. | Messrs.____:wholesale chemists |
| Q - 3. GALLOWS | C. | Setting of novel |
| N - 4. JEKYLL | D. | Sir Danvers Carew was a member of _____. |
| I - 5. EIGHT | E. | ____Square: location of Dr. Lanyon's home |
| O - 6. DENMAN | F. | Footman |
| S - 7. SIX | G. | Pounds Mr. Hyde gave the family |
| W - 8. JOHN | H. | Witnessed the murder |
| R - 9. GABRIEL | I. | ____or ten: trampled girl's age |
| F - 10. BRADSHAW | J. | Disagreed with Dr. Jekyll's methods |
| M - 11. EDWARD | K. | Inspector |
| U - 12. RICHARD | L. | Time of murder/time the messenger came |
| A - 13. HASTIE | M. | Mr. Hyde's first name |
| E - 14. CAVENDISH | N. | Combination of good and evil |
| H - 15. MAID | O. | Surgical theater |
| P - 16. UTTERSON | P. | Dr. Jekyll's lawyer |
| C - 17. LONDON | Q. | Hyde feared this |
| K - 18. NEWCOMEN | R. | Mr. Utterson's first name |
| J - 19. LANYON | S. | Hours Dr. Jekyll could go before changing to Mr. Hyde |
| Y - 20. NINTH | T. | Dr. Lanyon held it for Dr. Jekyll |
| X - 21. TEN | U. | Mr. Enfield's first name |
| T - 22. DRAWER | V. | Dr. Lanyon felt this after his discovery |
| G - 23. ONE HUNDRED | W. | Mr. Utterson's middle name |
| B - 24. MAW | X. | # of years Dr. Lanyon had not seen Dr. Jekyll |
| V - 25. TERROR | Y. | Dr. Lanyon received the letter on this date |

Dr. Jekyll & Mr. Hyde Matching 4

___ 1. JEKYLL
___ 2. MIDNIGHT
___ 3. DANVERS
___ 4. JANUARY
___ 5. BRADSHAW
___ 6. WILL
___ 7. CHEQUE BOOK
___ 8. DENMAN
___ 9. EDINBURGH
___ 10. RED
___ 11. BLACK MAIL
___ 12. GABRIEL
___ 13. HATRED
___ 14. TERROR
___ 15. REGENT'S
___ 16. SOHO
___ 17. LONDON
___ 18. CAVENDISH
___ 19. SUNDAY
___ 20. HARRY
___ 21. NINTH
___ 22. GUEST
___ 23. SIX
___ 24. SCOTLAND
___ 25. PURPLE

A. Surgical theater
B. Mr. Utterson took it from the fire
C. Mr. Utterson's first name
D. Dr. Lanyon felt this after his discovery
E. Dr. Lanyon received the letter on this date
F. Mr. Utterson had Dr. Jekyll's
G. Second color of the liquid
H. First color of the liquid
I. Identified similarity in writings
J. Dr. Jekyll and Mr. Hyde felt this for each other
K. Hours Dr. Jekyll could go before changing to Mr. Hyde
L. ____Square: location of Dr. Lanyon's home
M. ____House: Mr. Enfield's name for the residence
N. Location of Mr. Hyde's house
O. ____Park: Dr. Jekyll involuntarily changed to Mr. Hyde here
P. Dr. Jekyll's accent
Q. Combination of good and evil
R. The Inspector worked at____Yard
S. First name of murdered man
T. Dr. Jekyll's nickname
U. Setting of novel
V. Mr. Utterson and Mr. Enfield's walking day
W. Time of murder/time the messenger came
X. Mr. Utterson dined at Dr. Jekyll's in this month
Y. Footman

Dr. Jekyll & Mr. Hyde Matching 4 Answer Key

| | | | |
|---|---|---|---|
| Q - 1. | JEKYLL | A. | Surgical theater |
| W - 2. | MIDNIGHT | B. | Mr. Utterson took it from the fire |
| S - 3. | DANVERS | C. | Mr. Utterson's first name |
| X - 4. | JANUARY | D. | Dr. Lanyon felt this after his discovery |
| Y - 5. | BRADSHAW | E. | Dr. Lanyon received the letter on this date |
| F - 6. | WILL | F. | Mr. Utterson had Dr. Jekyll's |
| B - 7. | CHEQUE BOOK | G. | Second color of the liquid |
| A - 8. | DENMAN | H. | First color of the liquid |
| P - 9. | EDINBURGH | I. | Identified similarity in writings |
| H -10. | RED | J. | Dr. Jekyll and Mr. Hyde felt this for each other |
| M -11. | BLACK MAIL | K. | Hours Dr. Jekyll could go before changing to Mr. Hyde |
| C -12. | GABRIEL | L. | ____Square: location of Dr. Lanyon's home |
| J -13. | HATRED | M. | ____House: Mr. Enfield's name for the residence |
| D -14. | TERROR | N. | Location of Mr. Hyde's house |
| O -15. | REGENT'S | O. | ____Park: Dr. Jekyll involuntarily changed to Mr. Hyde here |
| N -16. | SOHO | P. | Dr. Jekyll's accent |
| U -17. | LONDON | Q. | Combination of good and evil |
| L -18. | CAVENDISH | R. | The Inspector worked at_____Yard |
| V -19. | SUNDAY | S. | First name of murdered man |
| T -20. | HARRY | T. | Dr. Jekyll's nickname |
| E -21. | NINTH | U. | Setting of novel |
| I -22. | GUEST | V. | Mr. Utterson and Mr. Enfield's walking day |
| K -23. | SIX | W. | Time of murder/time the messenger came |
| R -24. | SCOTLAND | X. | Mr. Utterson dined at Dr. Jekyll's in this month |
| G -25. | PURPLE | Y. | Footman |

Dr. Jekyll & Mr. Hyde Magic Squares 1

Match the definition with the vocabulary word. Put your answers in the magic squares below. When your answers are correct, all columns and rows will add to the same number.

| | | | |
|---|---|---|---|
| A. LANYON | E. PORTLAND | I. SCOTLAND | M. ONE HUNDRED |
| B. POOLE | F. TEN | J. GALLOWS | N. GAIETY |
| C. JEKYLL | G. MAW | K. JANUARY | O. RED |
| D. THREE | H. EDWARD | L. UTTERSON | P. SUNDAY |

1. Disagreed with Dr. Jekyll's methods
2. Dr. Jekyll didn't like it about himself
3. Hyde feared this
4. ____ Street: Mr. Hyde drove to a hotel there
5. Messrs. ____ :wholesale chemists
6. Dr. Jekyll's lawyer
7. Mr. Utterson and Mr. Enfield's walking day
8. Combination of good and evil
9. First color of the liquid
10. AM time when girl was trampled
11. Mr. Hyde's first name
12. Mr. Utterson dined at Dr. Jekyll's in this month
13. The Inspector worked at ____ Yard
14. # of years Dr. Lanyon had not seen Dr. Jekyll
15. Dr. Jekyll's servant
16. Pounds Mr. Hyde gave the family

| | | | |
|---|---|---|---|
| A= | B= | C= | D= |
| E= | F= | G= | H= |
| I= | J= | K= | L= |
| M= | N= | O= | P= |

Dr. Jekyll & Mr. Hyde Magic Squares 1 Answer Key

Match the definition with the vocabulary word. Put your answers in the magic squares below. When your answers are correct, all columns and rows will add to the same number.

A. LANYON  
B. POOLE  
C. JEKYLL  
D. THREE  
E. PORTLAND  
F. TEN  
G. MAW  
H. EDWARD  
I. SCOTLAND  
J. GALLOWS  
K. JANUARY  
L. UTTERSON  
M. ONE HUNDRED  
N. GAIETY  
O. RED  
P. SUNDAY  

1. Disagreed with Dr. Jekyll's methods
2. Dr. Jekyll didn't like it about himself
3. Hyde feared this
4. ____ Street: Mr. Hyde drove to a hotel there
5. Messrs.____:wholesale chemists
6. Dr. Jekyll's lawyer
7. Mr. Utterson and Mr. Enfield's walking day
8. Combination of good and evil
9. First color of the liquid
10. AM time when girl was trampled
11. Mr. Hyde's first name
12. Mr. Utterson dined at Dr. Jekyll's in this month
13. The Inspector worked at_____Yard
14. # of years Dr. Lanyon had not seen Dr. Jekyll
15. Dr. Jekyll's servant
16. Pounds Mr. Hyde gave the family

| A=1 | B=15 | C=8 | D=10 |
|---|---|---|---|
| E=4 | F=14 | G=5 | H=11 |
| I=13 | J=3 | K=12 | L=6 |
| M=16 | N=2 | O=9 | P=7 |

Dr. Jekyll & Mr. Hyde Magic Squares 2

Match the definition with the vocabulary word. Put your answers in the magic squares below. When your answers are correct, all columns and rows will add to the same number.

A. NEWCOMEN
B. CAVENDISH
C. HARRY
D. GREEN
E. RICHARD
F. GAIETY
G. HENRY
H. EDWARD
I. BRADSHAW
J. BLACK MAIL
K. MAID
L. LONDON
M. WILL
N. GABRIEL
O. SCOTLAND
P. JANUARY

1. Mr. Utterson had Dr. Jekyll's
2. Dr. Jekyll didn't like it about himself
3. Mr. Hyde's first name
4. The Inspector worked at _____ Yard
5. Setting of novel
6. Dr. Jekyll's nickname
7. Inspector
8. _____ House: Mr. Enfield's name for the residence
9. Witnessed the murder
10. Third color of the liquid/cheque book color
11. _____ Square: location of Dr. Lanyon's home
12. Footman
13. Mr. Utterson's first name
14. Mr. Enfield's first name
15. Dr. Jekyll's first name
16. Mr. Utterson dined at Dr. Jekyll's in this month

| A= | B= | C= | D= |
| E= | F= | G= | H= |
| I= | J= | K= | L= |
| M= | N= | O= | P= |

23
Copyrighted

Dr. Jekyll & Mr. Hyde Magic Squares 2 Answer Key

Match the definition with the vocabulary word. Put your answers in the magic squares below. When your answers are correct, all columns and rows will add to the same number.

A. NEWCOMEN
B. CAVENDISH
C. HARRY
D. GREEN
E. RICHARD
F. GAIETY
G. HENRY
H. EDWARD
I. BRADSHAW
J. BLACK MAIL
K. MAID
L. LONDON
M. WILL
N. GABRIEL
O. SCOTLAND
P. JANUARY

1. Mr. Utterson had Dr. Jekyll's
2. Dr. Jekyll didn't like it about himself
3. Mr. Hyde's first name
4. The Inspector worked at _____ Yard
5. Setting of novel
6. Dr. Jekyll's nickname
7. Inspector
8. ____House: Mr. Enfield's name for the residence
9. Witnessed the murder
10. Third color of the liquid/cheque book color
11. ____Square: location of Dr. Lanyon's home
12. Footman
13. Mr. Utterson's first name
14. Mr. Enfield's first name
15. Dr. Jekyll's first name
16. Mr. Utterson dined at Dr. Jekyll's in this month

| A=7 | B=11 | C=6 | D=10 |
| --- | --- | --- | --- |
| E=14 | F=2 | G=15 | H=3 |
| I=12 | J=8 | K=9 | L=5 |
| M=1 | N=13 | O=4 | P=16 |

Dr. Jekyll & Mr. Hyde Magic Squares 3

Match the definition with the vocabulary word. Put your answers in the magic squares below. When your answers are correct, all columns and rows will add to the same number.

| | | | |
|---|---|---|---|
| A. SIX | E. ONE HUNDRED | I. POOLE | M. PORTLAND |
| B. GREEN | F. CAVENDISH | J. WALKS | N. BLACK MAIL |
| C. MIDNIGHT | G. SOHO | K. MAW | O. EDWARD |
| D. HOUSEKEEPER | H. WILL | L. RED | P. SUNDAY |

1. Mr. Utterson had Dr. Jekyll's
2. Hours Dr. Jekyll could go before changing to Mr. Hyde
3. Third color of the liquid/cheque book color
4. Location of Mr. Hyde's house
5. Mr. Utterson and Mr. Enfield took them
6. Mr. Hyde's first name
7. Mr. Utterson and Mr. Enfield's walking day
8. Dr. Jekyll's servant
9. Messrs.____:wholesale chemists
10. ____House: Mr. Enfield's name for the residence
11. ____ Street: Mr. Hyde drove to a hotel there
12. First color of the liquid
13. Pounds Mr. Hyde gave the family
14. Was glad Mr. Hyde was in trouble
15. Time of murder/time the messenger came
16. ____Square: location of Dr. Lanyon's home

| A= | B= | C= | D= |
|---|---|---|---|
| E= | F= | G= | H= |
| I= | J= | K= | L= |
| M= | N= | O= | P= |

Dr. Jekyll & Mr. Hyde Magic Squares 3 Answer Key

Match the definition with the vocabulary word. Put your answers in the magic squares below. When your answers are correct, all columns and rows will add to the same number.

A. SIX  
B. GREEN  
C. MIDNIGHT  
D. HOUSEKEEPER  
E. ONE HUNDRED  
F. CAVENDISH  
G. SOHO  
H. WILL  
I. POOLE  
J. WALKS  
K. MAW  
L. RED  
M. PORTLAND  
N. BLACK MAIL  
O. EDWARD  
P. SUNDAY  

1. Mr. Utterson had Dr. Jekyll's
2. Hours Dr. Jekyll could go before changing to Mr. Hyde
3. Third color of the liquid/cheque book color
4. Location of Mr. Hyde's house
5. Mr. Utterson and Mr. Enfield took them
6. Mr. Hyde's first name
7. Mr. Utterson and Mr. Enfield's walking day
8. Dr. Jekyll's servant
9. Messrs.____:wholesale chemists
10. ____House: Mr. Enfield's name for the residence
11. ____ Street: Mr. Hyde drove to a hotel there
12. First color of the liquid
13. Pounds Mr. Hyde gave the family
14. Was glad Mr. Hyde was in trouble
15. Time of murder/time the messenger came
16. ____Square: location of Dr. Lanyon's home

| A=2 | B=3 | C=15 | D=14 |
| E=13 | F=16 | G=4 | H=1 |
| I=8 | J=5 | K=9 | L=12 |
| M=11 | N=10 | O=6 | P=7 |

Dr. Jekyll & Mr. Hyde Magic Squares 4

Match the definition with the vocabulary word. Put your answers in the magic squares below. When your answers are correct, all columns and rows will add to the same number.

A. HOUSEKEEPER
B. SIX
C. PURPLE
D. HASTIE
E. THREE
F. EDWARD
G. GUEST
H. SOHO
I. LANYON
J. SUNDAY
K. TEN
L. GREEN
M. CANE
N. NINTH
O. PORTLAND
P. CHEQUE BOOK

1. Location of Mr. Hyde's house
2. Murder weapon
3. Hours Dr. Jekyll could go before changing to Mr. Hyde
4. # of years Dr. Lanyon had not seen Dr. Jekyll
5. Mr. Utterson and Mr. Enfield's walking day
6. Second color of the liquid
7. Mr. Utterson took it from the fire
8. AM time when girl was trampled
9. ____ Street: Mr. Hyde drove to a hotel there
10. Mr. Hyde's first name
11. Disagreed with Dr. Jekyll's methods
12. Dr. Lanyon's first name
13. Was glad Mr. Hyde was in trouble
14. Third color of the liquid/cheque book color
15. Identified similarity in writings
16. Dr. Lanyon received the letter on this date

| A= | B= | C= | D= |
| E= | F= | G= | H= |
| I= | J= | K= | L= |
| M= | N= | O= | P= |

Dr. Jekyll & Mr. Hyde Magic Squares 4 Answer Key

Match the definition with the vocabulary word. Put your answers in the magic squares below. When your answers are correct, all columns and rows will add to the same number.

A. HOUSEKEEPER
B. SIX
C. PURPLE
D. HASTIE
E. THREE
F. EDWARD
G. GUEST
H. SOHO
I. LANYON
J. SUNDAY
K. TEN
L. GREEN
M. CANE
N. NINTH
O. PORTLAND
P. CHEQUE BOOK

1. Location of Mr. Hyde's house
2. Murder weapon
3. Hours Dr. Jekyll could go before changing to Mr. Hyde
4. # of years Dr. Lanyon had not seen Dr. Jekyll
5. Mr. Utterson and Mr. Enfield's walking day
6. Second color of the liquid
7. Mr. Utterson took it from the fire
8. AM time when girl was trampled
9. ____ Street: Mr. Hyde drove to a hotel there
10. Mr. Hyde's first name
11. Disagreed with Dr. Jekyll's methods
12. Dr. Lanyon's first name
13. Was glad Mr. Hyde was in trouble
14. Third color of the liquid/cheque book color
15. Identified similarity in writings
16. Dr. Lanyon received the letter on this date

| A=13 | B=3 | C=6 | D=12 |
| --- | --- | --- | --- |
| E=8 | F=10 | G=15 | H=1 |
| I=11 | J=5 | K=4 | L=14 |
| M=2 | N=16 | O=9 | P=7 |

# Dr. Jekyll & Mr. Hyde Word Search 1

```
P A R L I A M E N T G A L L O W S K E Z
S C O T L A N D M K L C T H G I N D I M
H W Y Q H R S E X Q A H D R U G S W G Q
A M R S S J U N J X N A L L Y K E J H B
T N R M I Z N M S Z Y S K F R N M S T Q
R B A L D Z D A O G O T N W A C ' Y Q Y
E I H T N N A N H P N I D I U T A Z R R
D R A W E R Y R O R R E T L N O D N O L
H F N E V N R O P N R D D E A E E W E D
T T R Y A B L F R G L L G W J H T E U F
P G Z S C E R G W K A E D Q A R E Y T S
P B L A C K M A I L R I C H A R D C T Z
T U L Q P S L B D D L F E R H B D S E C
Z P R F S K J R X S X N D T G X E Q R D
L V J P S I H I H B H E K J Y U R J S J
W I L L L G X E D Y H A C W G M J J O F
P V M L W E Q L N Q W Z W R Q A Y H N M
N I N T H D A N V E R S W Q T W N W C W
```

Mr. Utterson and Mr. Enfield's walking day (6)
Second color of the liquid (6)
____Square: location of Dr. Lanyon's home (9)
# of years Dr. Lanyon had not seen Dr. Jekyll (3)
AM time when girl was trampled (5)
Caused the change from Jekyll to Hyde (5)
Combination of good and evil (6)
Disagreed with Dr. Jekyll's methods (6)
Dr. Jekyll and Mr. Hyde felt this for each other (6)
Dr. Jekyll didn't like it about himself (6)
Dr. Jekyll's first name (5)
Dr. Jekyll's lawyer (8)
Dr. Jekyll's nickname (5)
Dr. Jekyll's servant (5)
Dr. Lanyon felt this after his discovery (6)
Dr. Lanyon held it for Dr. Jekyll (6)
Dr. Lanyon received the letter on this date (5)
Dr. Lanyon's first name (6)
First color of the liquid (3)
First name of murdered man (7)
Footman (8)
Hours Dr. Jekyll could go before changing to Mr. Hyde (3)
Hyde feared this (7)
Identified similarity in writings (5)

Location of Mr. Hyde's house (4)
Messrs.____:wholesale chemists (3)
Mr. Enfield's first name (7)
Mr. Hyde's first name (6)
Mr. Utterson and Mr. Enfield took them (5)
Mr. Utterson dined at Dr. Jekyll's in this month (7)
Mr. Utterson had Dr. Jekyll's (4)
Mr. Utterson's first name (7)
Mr. Utterson's middle name (4)
Murder weapon (4)
Pounds for which the cheque was written (6)
Pure evil (4)
Saw Mr. Hyde trample a girl (7)
Setting of novel (6)
Sir Danvers Carew was a member of _____. (10)
Surgical theater (6)
The Inspector worked at____Yard (8)
Third color of the liquid/cheque book color (5)
Witnessed the murder (4)
____House: Mr. Enfield's name for the residence (10)
____Park: Dr. Jekyll involuntarily changed to Mr. Hyde here (8)
____or ten: trampled girl's age (5)
Time of murder/time the messenger came (8)

Dr. Jekyll & Mr. Hyde Word Search 1 Answer Key

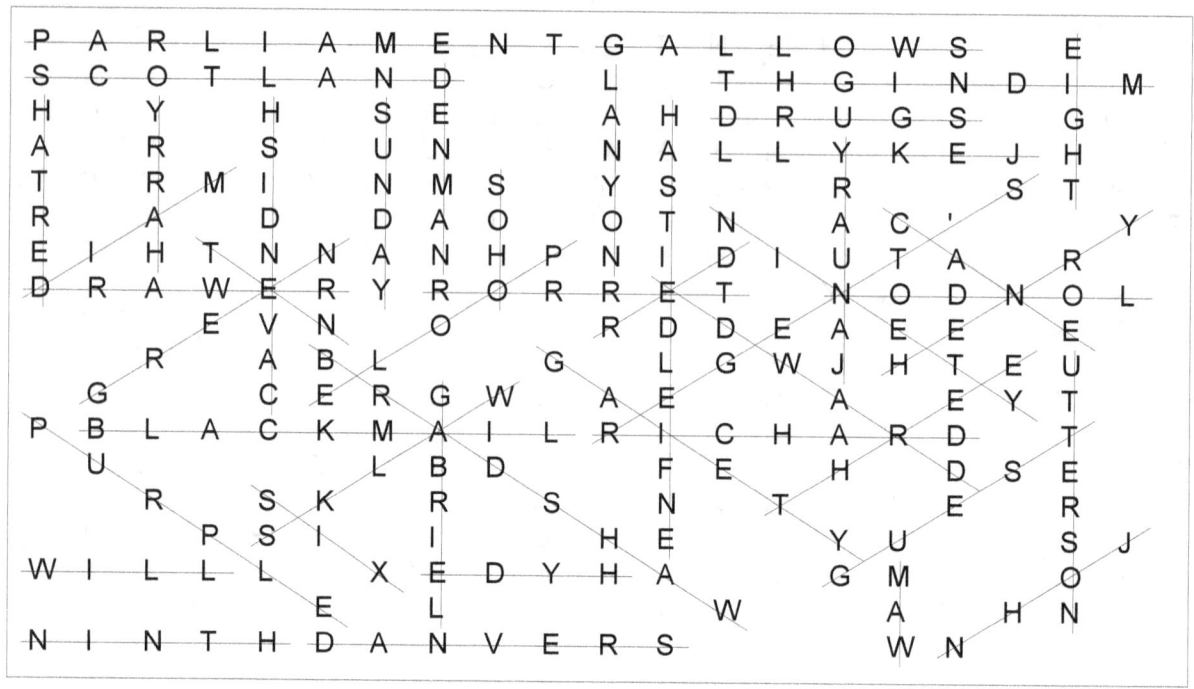

Mr. Utterson and Mr. Enfield's walking day (6)
Second color of the liquid (6)
____Square: location of Dr. Lanyon's home (9)
# of years Dr. Lanyon had not seen Dr. Jekyll (3)
AM time when girl was trampled (5)
Caused the change from Jekyll to Hyde (5)
Combination of good and evil (6)
Disagreed with Dr. Jekyll's methods (6)
Dr. Jekyll and Mr. Hyde felt this for each other (6)
Dr. Jekyll didn't like it about himself (6)
Dr. Jekyll's first name (5)
Dr. Jekyll's lawyer (8)
Dr. Jekyll's nickname (5)
Dr. Jekyll's servant (5)
Dr. Lanyon felt this after his discovery (6)
Dr. Lanyon held it for Dr. Jekyll (6)
Dr. Lanyon received the letter on this date (5)
Dr. Lanyon's first name (6)
First color of the liquid (3)
First name of murdered man (7)
Footman (8)
Hours Dr. Jekyll could go before changing to Mr. Hyde (3)
Hyde feared this (7)
Identified similarity in writings (5)

Location of Mr. Hyde's house (4)
Messrs.____:wholesale chemists (3)
Mr. Enfield's first name (7)
Mr. Hyde's first name (6)
Mr. Utterson and Mr. Enfield took them (5)
Mr. Utterson dined at Dr. Jekyll's in this month (7)
Mr. Utterson had Dr. Jekyll's (4)
Mr. Utterson's first name (7)
Mr. Utterson's middle name (4)
Murder weapon (4)
Pounds for which the cheque was written (6)
Pure evil (4)
Saw Mr. Hyde trample a girl (7)
Setting of novel (6)
Sir Danvers Carew was a member of _____. (10)
Surgical theater (6)
The Inspector worked at_____Yard (8)
Third color of the liquid/cheque book color (5)
Witnessed the murder (4)
____House: Mr. Enfield's name for the residence (10)
____Park: Dr. Jekyll involuntarily changed to Mr. Hyde here (8)
____or ten: trampled girl's age (5)
Time of murder/time the messenger came (8)

# Dr. Jekyll & Mr. Hyde Word Search 2

```
H E N R Y C R S E I G H T H G I N D I M
O A T F K O W N N X R R G Y P R R A H Z
U V T M R O F H A D W R E D K U Y N R J
S N Z R L I Y O C A U J F E G N X V W M
E G E L E V L J H B Q A C S N I W E M H
K T A L D D L S N Q N N T ' W N D R S W
E G D Y W W D I U T G U I T M E L S K N
E P M L A A D T T G H A G N P T L T L C
P O W D R E T L L S F R J E T Y R R A H
E R Y B D E L P R U P Y E G G H C T W T
R T J D R I D H L S L S W E P F A X Q K
L L J S W R N L A N Y O N R J S V L T B
H A O E A D R A W E R H R Y E Q E Q K C
V N G H K H E C N I T O T L Y I N X D G
F D C C Q Y Z N M T L E O Y R R D B U N
L I T C R Z L A M S I O B B E H I E V P
R T N E M A I L R A P Y A D N U S I X D
P P L O N D O N G H N G M A W T H Y D E
```

Mr. Utterson and Mr. Enfield's walking day (6)
Second color of the liquid (6)
____Square: location of Dr. Lanyon's home (9)
# of years Dr. Lanyon had not seen Dr. Jekyll (3)
AM time when girl was trampled (5)
Caused the change from Jekyll to Hyde (5)
Combination of good and evil (6)
Disagreed with Dr. Jekyll's methods (6)
Dr. Jekyll and Mr. Hyde felt this for each other (6)
Dr. Jekyll didn't like it about himself (6)
Dr. Jekyll's accent (9)
Dr. Jekyll's first name (5)
Dr. Jekyll's lawyer (8)
Dr. Jekyll's nickname (5)
Dr. Jekyll's servant (5)
Dr. Lanyon felt this after his discovery (6)
Dr. Lanyon held it for Dr. Jekyll (6)
Dr. Lanyon received the letter on this date (5)
Dr. Lanyon's first name (6)
First color of the liquid (3)
First name of murdered man (7)
Footman (8)
Hours Dr. Jekyll could go before changing to Mr. Hyde (3)
Hyde feared this (7)
Identified similarity in writings (5)
Location of Mr. Hyde's house (4)
Messrs.____:wholesale chemists (3)
Mr. Enfield's first name (7)
Mr. Hyde's first name (6)
Mr. Utterson and Mr. Enfield took them (5)
Mr. Utterson dined at Dr. Jekyll's in this month (7)
Mr. Utterson had Dr. Jekyll's (4)
Mr. Utterson's first name (7)
Mr. Utterson's middle name (4)
Murder weapon (4)
Pounds fro which the cheque was written (6)
Pure evil (4)
Saw Mr. Hyde trample a girl (7)
Setting of novel (6)
Sir Danvers Carew was a member of _____. (10)
Surgical theater (6)
Third color of the liquid/cheque book color (5)
Was glad Mr. Hyde was in trouble (11)
Witnessed the murder (4)
____ Street: Mr. Hyde drove to a hotel there (8)
____Park: Dr. Jekyll involuntarily changed to Mr. Hyde here (8)
____or ten: trampled girl's age (5)
Time of murder/time the messenger came (8)

# Dr. Jekyll & Mr. Hyde Word Search 2 Answer Key

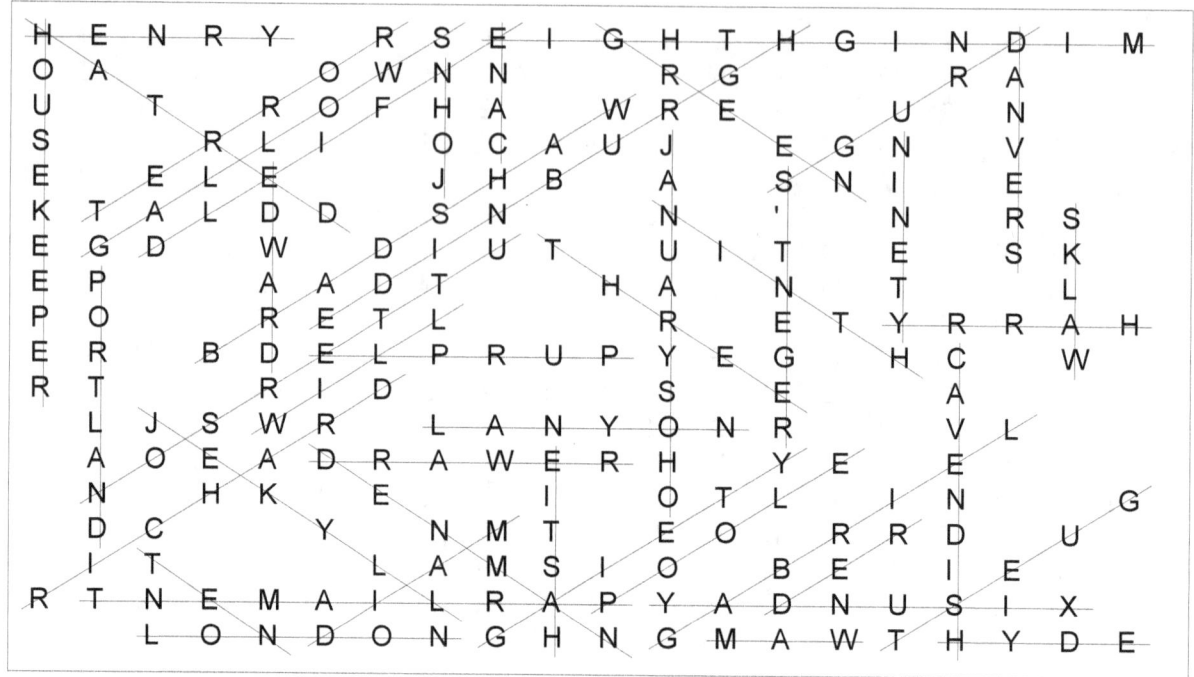

Mr. Utterson and Mr. Enfield's walking day (6)
Second color of the liquid (6)
____Square: location of Dr. Lanyon's home (9)
# of years Dr. Lanyon had not seen Dr. Jekyll (3)
AM time when girl was trampled (5)
Caused the change from Jekyll to Hyde (5)
Combination of good and evil (6)
Disagreed with Dr. Jekyll's methods (6)
Dr. Jekyll and Mr. Hyde felt this for each other (6)
Dr. Jekyll didn't like it about himself (6)
Dr. Jekyll's accent (9)
Dr. Jekyll's first name (5)
Dr. Jekyll's lawyer (8)
Dr. Jekyll's nickname (5)
Dr. Jekyll's servant (5)
Dr. Lanyon felt this after his discovery (6)
Dr. Lanyon held it for Dr. Jekyll (6)
Dr. Lanyon received the letter on this date (5)
Dr. Lanyon's first name (6)
First color of the liquid (3)
First name of murdered man (7)
Footman (8)
Hours Dr. Jekyll could go before changing to Mr. Hyde (3)
Hyde feared this (7)

Identified similarity in writings (5)
Location of Mr. Hyde's house (4)
Messrs.____:wholesale chemists (3)
Mr. Enfield's first name (7)
Mr. Hyde's first name (6)
Mr. Utterson and Mr. Enfield took them (5)
Mr. Utterson dined at Dr. Jekyll's in this month (7)
Mr. Utterson had Dr. Jekyll's (4)
Mr. Utterson's first name (7)
Mr. Utterson's middle name (4)
Murder weapon (4)
Pounds for which the cheque was written (6)
Pure evil (4)
Saw Mr. Hyde trample a girl (7)
Setting of novel (6)
Sir Danvers Carew was a member of _____. (10)
Surgical theater (6)
Third color of the liquid/cheque book color (5)
Was glad Mr. Hyde was in trouble (11)
Witnessed the murder (4)
____ Street: Mr. Hyde drove to a hotel there (8)
____Park: Dr. Jekyll involuntarily changed to Mr. Hyde here (8)
____or ten: trampled girl's age (5)
Time of murder/time the messenger came (8)

# Dr. Jekyll & Mr. Hyde Word Search 3

```
L L W L B C H E Q U E B O O K M T Z S M
G H Z S R Y J K Y D S Y X R P W N W S O
Z G T M Q P Y S K X Z H G Q G W Q P N P
Y P S P O R T L A N D P K A V N F E X P
G V C Y Z R D F Y P D G L X X F H R G R
L Z O D G E J K S T X L H J H U X T O X
B J T R N N L ' X T O X A G N W Y R G S
U L L M W I T G N W E D T D U Y R P W P
T C A V E N D I S H E N R Y T E I A G W
T N N C E T Y J Y G O E E U T H S R T X
E L D G K H F D M R D U D S G F R T H D
R C E D G M E K Y U J N S M I S M E R D
S R D L E N A C R B G R E E N X W A E M
O O L N O Y Y I R N X J I I K A W R I Z
N I H Y Z N C A L I J J T G M E N J B D
W O N O E H D B D D F R S H R D E Y B C
J A C L A S E O N E M S A T J A H P J M
L J O R H L D E N I K E H B E N A W E K
C O D A P L M D L N T N Y K V R M W R
P T W R S O P N A F M E R G Y E R G S V
G G U G C U I W I X G A T R L R Y V R D
P P B W R G N E T Y U P S Y L S K W L L
Y R E L H Y L D G N S D F W G L C J L R
J N H T G D B G A B R I E L E D W A R D
M N P H Q Y K J H Y P A R L I A M E N T
```

| | | | | |
|---|---|---|---|---|
| BLACK MAIL | EIGHT | HOUSEKEEPER | NINETY | SIX |
| BRADSHAW | ENFIELD | HYDE | NINTH | SOHO |
| CANE | GABRIEL | JANUARY | ONE HUNDRED | SUNDAY |
| CAVENDISH | GAIETY | JEKYLL | PARLIAMENT | TEN |
| CHEQUE BOOK | GALLOWS | JOHN | POOLE | TERROR |
| DANVERS | GREEN | LANYON | PORTLAND | THREE |
| DENMAN | GUEST | LONDON | PURPLE | UTTERSON |
| DRAWER | HARRY | MAID | RED | WALKS |
| DRUGS | HASTIE | MAW | REGENT'S | WILL |
| EDINBURGH | HATRED | MIDNIGHT | RICHARD | |
| EDWARD | HENRY | NEWCOMEN | SCOTLAND | |

Dr. Jekyll & Mr. Hyde Word Search 3 Answer Key

| BLACK MAIL | EIGHT | HOUSEKEEPER | NINETY | SIX |
| BRADSHAW | ENFIELD | HYDE | NINTH | SOHO |
| CANE | GABRIEL | JANUARY | ONE HUNDRED | SUNDAY |
| CAVENDISH | GAIETY | JEKYLL | PARLIAMENT | TEN |
| CHEQUE BOOK | GALLOWS | JOHN | POOLE | TERROR |
| DANVERS | GREEN | LANYON | PORTLAND | THREE |
| DENMAN | GUEST | LONDON | PURPLE | UTTERSON |
| DRAWER | HARRY | MAID | RED | WALKS |
| DRUGS | HASTIE | MAW | REGENT'S | WILL |
| EDINBURGH | HATRED | MIDNIGHT | RICHARD | |
| EDWARD | HENRY | NEWCOMEN | SCOTLAND | |

# Dr. Jekyll & Mr. Hyde Word Search 4

```
J A N U A R Y G C N V L U N T S E U G C
R C A V E N D I S H R Q Y T H I E C S L
S D V C N B S ' T N E G E R T X L A O J
Y N W T W R M G K R N Q M S H E P N H C
P A R L I A M E N T V H U Z J Y R E O N
M L R W I D L Y K B H N H E R X U S Z L
K T L D D S B K L L D W G R B V P C O L
Z O W J K H P K S A N P A E S O R Z V N
Y C F N A A C C Y C A H L W P O O F S B
J S R T D W K S J K L B M A R Q H K N S
Q J R J N L P C T M T V P R R H V O R D
N E E R G R I C H A R D E D C C Y E P T
D K S W O L L A G I O T D S E N V D D C
T Y Z Y O Q S F I L P K I M A N P V E W
Y L W N Q Q F M E H T P N L A N M M G H
Y L D K C S I F V N E C B D D R C A O S
C O F M B D P R E M N N U E W P M U N N
N S R N N N H M E D W A R D H A S T I E
I J C I S S O Y L Z L D G Y E E J N P K
N J G Y R C Z P M E N R H L K V T Q S G
E H M T W E D H I U D L O E X H Y R M G
T H R E E G D R H F N O E D L E I F N E
Y W N I Z D B E U E P P P L C T S H K S
B S C A H A N K T G E Y I Q C X O S D S
Q C S G G O S V V R S W J M P J Q L N S
```

BLACK MAIL    EIGHT       HOUSEKEEPER   NINETY        SIX
BRADSHAW      ENFIELD     HYDE          NINTH         SOHO
CANE          GABRIEL     JANUARY       ONE HUNDRED   SUNDAY
CAVENDISH     GAIETY      JEKYLL        PARLIAMENT    TEN
CHEQUE BOOK   GALLOWS     JOHN          POOLE         TERROR
DANVERS       GREEN       LANYON        PORTLAND      THREE
DENMAN        GUEST       LONDON        PURPLE        UTTERSON
DRAWER        HARRY       MAID          RED           WALKS
DRUGS         HASTIE      MAW           REGENT'S      WILL
EDINBURGH     HATRED      MIDNIGHT      RICHARD
EDWARD        HENRY       NEWCOMEN      SCOTLAND

# Dr. Jekyll & Mr. Hyde Word Search 4 Answer Key

| BLACK MAIL | EIGHT | HOUSEKEEPER | NINETY | SIX |
| --- | --- | --- | --- | --- |
| BRADSHAW | ENFIELD | HYDE | NINTH | SOHO |
| CANE | GABRIEL | JANUARY | ONE HUNDRED | SUNDAY |
| CAVENDISH | GAIETY | JEKYLL | PARLIAMENT | TEN |
| CHEQUE BOOK | GALLOWS | JOHN | POOLE | TERROR |
| DANVERS | GREEN | LANYON | PORTLAND | THREE |
| DENMAN | GUEST | LONDON | PURPLE | UTTERSON |
| DRAWER | HARRY | MAID | RED | WALKS |
| DRUGS | HASTIE | MAW | REGENT'S | WILL |
| EDINBURGH | HATRED | MIDNIGHT | RICHARD | |
| EDWARD | HENRY | NEWCOMEN | SCOTLAND | |

# Dr. Jekyll & Mr. Hyde Crossword 1

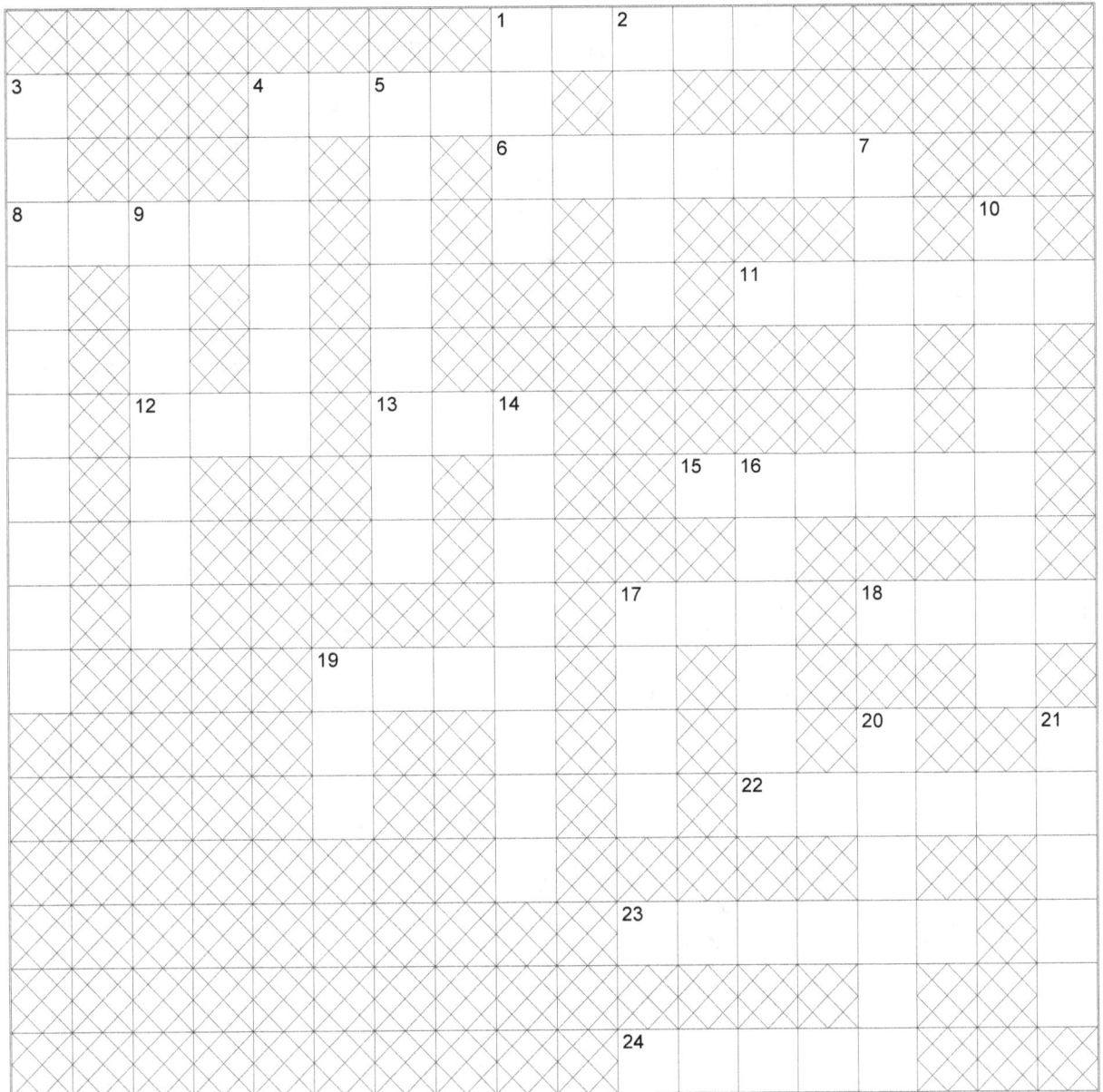

**Across**
1. Dr. Jekyll's first name
4. Dr. Jekyll's nickname
6. First name of murdered man
8. ____ or ten: trampled girl's age
11. Setting of novel
12. First color of the liquid
13. # of years Dr. Lanyon had not seen Dr. Jekyll
15. Combination of good and evil
17. Messrs.____:wholesale chemists
18. Murder weapon
19. Location of Mr. Hyde's house
22. Dr. Lanyon held it for Dr. Jekyll
23. Dr. Jekyll didn't like it about himself
24. Dr. Jekyll's servant

**Down**
1. Pure evil
2. Dr. Lanyon received the letter on this date
3. Pounds Mr. Hyde gave the family
4. Dr. Jekyll and Mr. Hyde felt this for each other
5. ____Park: Dr. Jekyll involuntarily changed to Mr. Hyde here
7. Mr. Utterson and Mr. Enfield's walking day
9. Mr. Utterson's first name
10. ____ Street: Mr. Hyde drove to a hotel there
14. Inspector
16. Mr. Hyde's first name
17. Witnessed the murder
19. Hours Dr. Jekyll could go before changing to Mr. Hyde
20. Dr. Lanyon's first name
21. Caused the change from Jekyll to Hyde

# Dr. Jekyll & Mr. Hyde Crossword 1 Answer Key

**Across**
1. Dr. Jekyll's first name
4. Dr. Jekyll's nickname
6. First name of murdered man
8. ____ or ten: trampled girl's age
11. Setting of novel
12. First color of the liquid
13. # of years Dr. Lanyon had not seen Dr. Jekyll
15. Combination of good and evil
17. Messrs.____:wholesale chemists
18. Murder weapon
19. Location of Mr. Hyde's house
22. Dr. Lanyon held it for Dr. Jekyll
23. Dr. Jekyll didn't like it about himself
24. Dr. Jekyll's servant

**Down**
1. Pure evil
2. Dr. Lanyon received the letter on this date
3. Pounds Mr. Hyde gave the family
4. Dr. Jekyll and Mr. Hyde felt this for each other
5. ____Park: Dr. Jekyll involuntarily changed to Mr. Hyde here
7. Mr. Utterson and Mr. Enfield's walking day
9. Mr. Utterson's first name
10. ____ Street: Mr. Hyde drove to a hotel there
14. Inspector
16. Mr. Hyde's first name
17. Witnessed the murder
19. Hours Dr. Jekyll could go before changing to Mr. Hyde
20. Dr. Lanyon's first name
21. Caused the change from Jekyll to Hyde

# Dr. Jekyll & Mr. Hyde Crossword 2

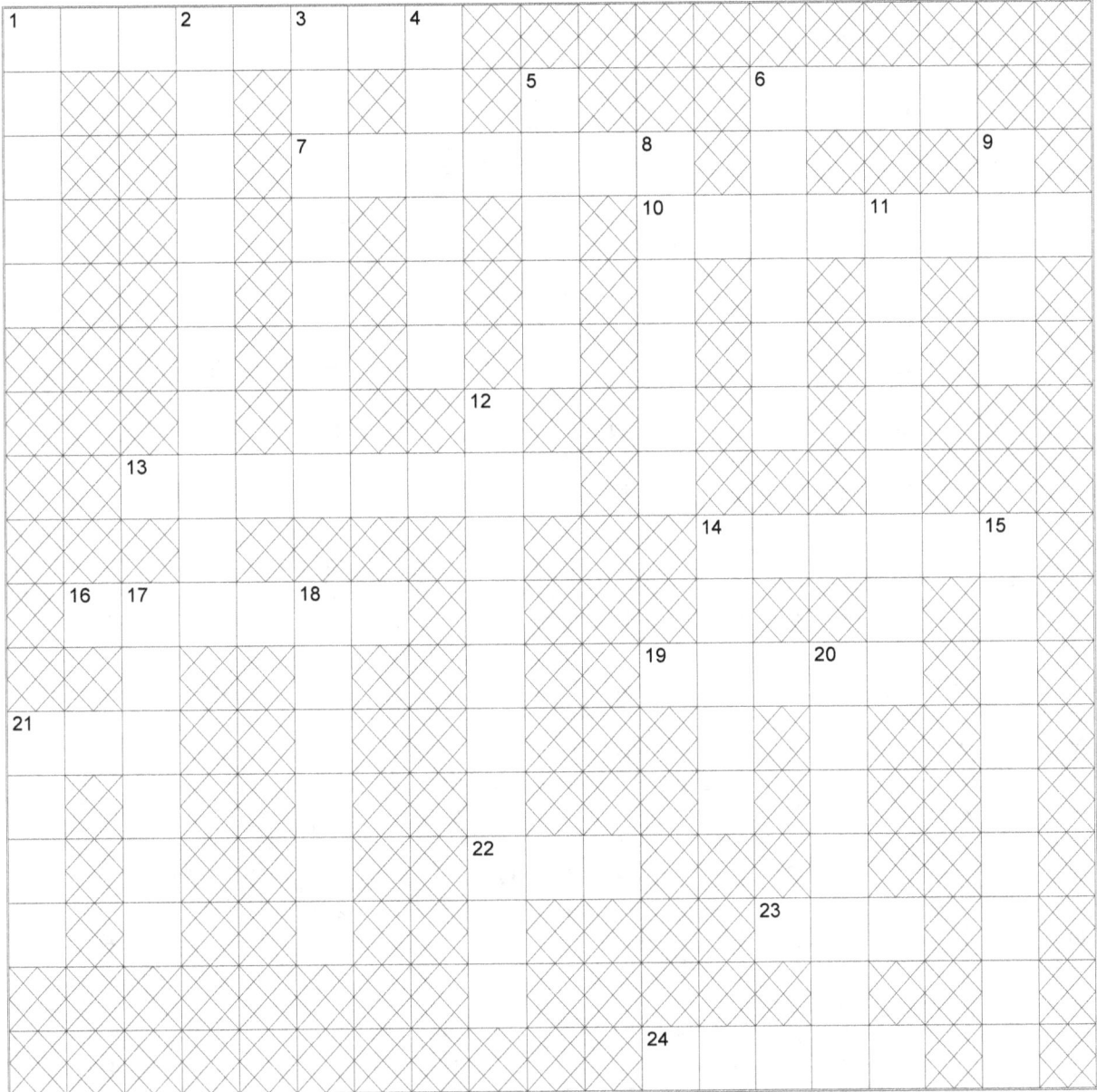

**Across**
1. Inspector
6. Pure evil
7. First name of murdered man
10. Dr. Jekyll's lawyer
13. ____ Street: Mr. Hyde drove to a hotel there
14. Dr. Lanyon's first name
16. Combination of good and evil
19. Caused the change from Jekyll to Hyde
21. Messrs.____:wholesale chemists
22. First color of the liquid
23. Hours Dr. Jekyll could go before changing to Mr. Hyde
24. Dr. Jekyll's servant

**Down**
1. Dr. Lanyon received the letter on this date
2. Mr. Utterson took it from the fire
3. Time of murder/time the messenger came
4. Pounds fro which the cheque was written
5. Dr. Jekyll's first name
6. Dr. Jekyll and Mr. Hyde felt this for each other
8. Mr. Utterson and Mr. Enfield's walking day
9. Mr. Utterson's middle name
11. ____Park: Dr. Jekyll involuntarily changed to Mr. Hyde here
12. Pounds Mr. Hyde gave the family
14. Dr. Jekyll's nickname
15. Dr. Jekyll's accent
17. Mr. Hyde's first name
18. Setting of novel
20. Mr. Utterson's first name
21. Witnessed the murder

# Dr. Jekyll & Mr. Hyde Crossword 2 Answer Key

|   | 1 N | E | W | 2 C | O | 3 M | E | 4 N |   |   |   |   |   |   |
|---|---|---|---|---|---|---|---|---|---|---|---|---|---|---|
|   | I |   |   | H |   | I |   | I |   | 5 H |   | 6 H | Y | D | E |
|   | N |   |   | E |   | 7 D | A | N | V | E | R | S | A |   | 9 J |
|   | T |   |   | Q |   | N |   | E |   | N |   | 10 U | T | 11 T | E | R | S | O | N |
|   | H |   |   | U |   | I |   | T |   | R |   | N |   | R |   | E |   |   | H |
|   |   |   |   | E |   | G |   | Y |   | Y |   | D |   | E |   | G |   |   | N |
|   |   |   |   | B |   | H |   |   | 12 O |   | A |   | D |   | E |   |   |   |
|   |   |   | 13 P | O | R | T | L | A | N | D |   | Y |   |   |   | N |   |   |   |
|   |   |   | O |   |   |   |   |   | E |   |   |   | 14 H | A | S | T | 15 I | E |
|   |   | 16 J | 17 E | K | Y | 18 L | L |   | H |   |   | A |   |   |   | ' |   | D |
|   |   |   | D |   |   | O |   |   | U |   | 19 D | R | U | 20 G | S |   | I |
|   | 21 M | A | W |   |   | N |   |   | N |   | R |   |   | A |   |   | N |
|   | A |   | A |   |   | D |   |   | D |   | Y |   |   | B |   |   | B |
|   | I |   | R |   |   | O |   | 22 R | E | D |   |   |   | R |   |   | U |
|   | D |   | D |   |   | N |   | E |   |   |   |   | 23 S | I | X |   | R |
|   |   |   |   |   |   |   |   | D |   |   |   |   | E |   |   | G |
|   |   |   |   |   |   |   |   | 24 P | O | O | L | E |   |   |   | H |

**Across**
1. Inspector
6. Pure evil
7. First name of murdered man
10. Dr. Jekyll's lawyer
13. ____ Street: Mr. Hyde drove to a hotel there
14. Dr. Lanyon's first name
16. Combination of good and evil
19. Caused the change from Jekyll to Hyde
21. Messrs.____:wholesale chemists
22. First color of the liquid
23. Hours Dr. Jekyll could go before changing to Mr. Hyde
24. Dr. Jekyll's servant

**Down**
1. Dr. Lanyon received the letter on this date
2. Mr. Utterson took it from the fire
3. Time of murder/time the messenger came
4. Pounds fro which the cheque was written
5. Dr. Jekyll's first name
6. Dr. Jekyll and Mr. Hyde felt this for each other
8. Mr. Utterson and Mr. Enfield's walking day
9. Mr. Utterson's middle name
11. ____Park: Dr. Jekyll involuntarily changed to Mr. Hyde here
12. Pounds Mr. Hyde gave the family
14. Dr. Jekyll's nickname
15. Dr. Jekyll's accent
17. Mr. Hyde's first name
18. Setting of novel
20. Mr. Utterson's first name
21. Witnessed the murder

# Dr. Jekyll & Mr. Hyde Crossword 3

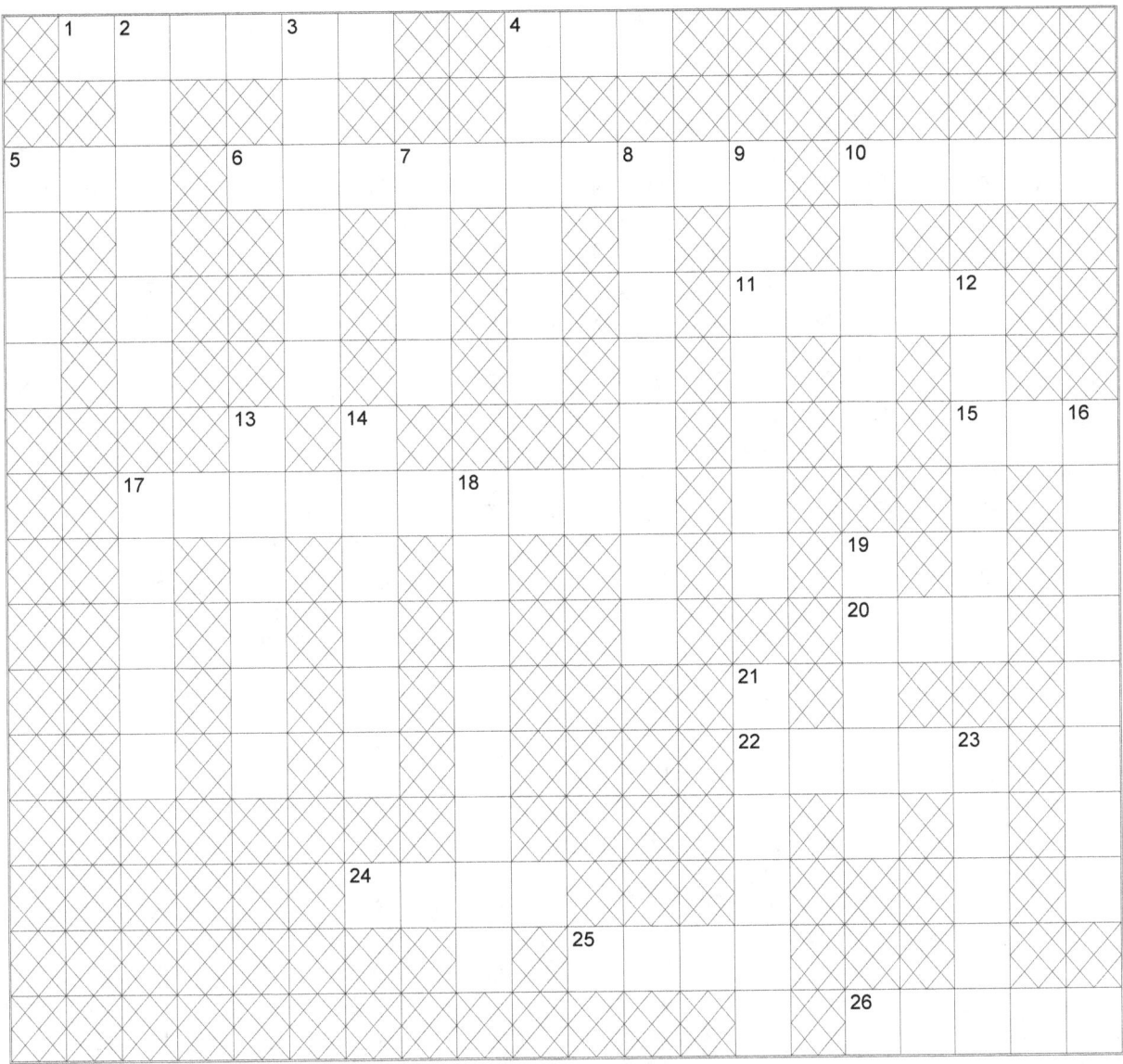

**Across**
1. Combination of good and evil
4. Hours Dr. Jekyll could go before changing to Mr. Hyde
5. Messrs.____:wholesale chemists
6. Pounds Mr. Hyde gave the family
10. Dr. Jekyll's nickname
11. Dr. Lanyon received the letter on this date
15. # of years Dr. Lanyon had not seen Dr. Jekyll
17. Sir Danvers Carew was a member of _____.
20. First color of the liquid
22. ____ or ten: trampled girl's age
24. Mr. Utterson's middle name
25. Location of Mr. Hyde's house
26. Third color of the liquid/cheque book color

**Down**
2. Mr. Hyde's first name
3. Setting of novel
4. Mr. Utterson and Mr. Enfield's walking day
5. Witnessed the murder
7. Pure evil
8. ____Park: Dr. Jekyll involuntarily changed to Mr. Hyde here
9. First name of murdered man
10. Dr. Jekyll's first name
12. Dr. Jekyll and Mr. Hyde felt this for each other
13. Dr. Lanyon held it for Dr. Jekyll
14. Pounds for which the cheque was written
16. Inspector
17. Dr. Jekyll's servant
18. Time of murder/time the messenger came
19. Caused the change from Jekyll to Hyde
21. Dr. Lanyon felt this after his discovery
23. AM time when girl was trampled

# Dr. Jekyll & Mr. Hyde Crossword 3 Answer Key

|   | 1 J | 2 E | K | Y | 3 L | L |   | 4 S | I | X |   |   |   |   |
|---|---|---|---|---|---|---|---|---|---|---|---|---|---|---|
|   |   | D |   |   | O |   |   | U |   |   |   |   |   |   |
| 5 M | A | W |   | 6 O | N | 7 E | H | U | N | 8 D | R | 9 E | 10 D | H | A | R | R | Y |
| A | A |   |   | A |   | D |   | Y |   | D |   | E |   |   |
| I | R |   |   | R |   | O |   | D |   | E |   | 11 N | I | 12 N | T | H |
| D | D |   |   | O |   | N |   | E |   | G |   | V |   | R |   | A |
|   |   |   | 13 D |   | 14 N |   |   | Y |   | E |   | E |   | 15 Y |   | 16 T | E | N |
|   |   | 17 P | A | R | L | I | 18 A | M | E | N | T |   | R |   |   | R |   | E |
|   |   | O |   | A |   | N |   | I |   |   | ' |   | S |   | 19 D |   | E |   | W |
|   |   | O |   | W |   | E |   | I | D |   |   |   | S |   | 20 R | E | D |   | C |
|   |   | L |   | E |   | T |   | N |   |   |   |   | 21 T |   | U |   |   |   | O |
|   |   | E |   | R |   | Y |   | I |   |   |   | 22 E | I | G | H | 23 T |   | M |
|   |   |   |   |   |   |   |   | G |   |   |   | R |   |   | S |   | H |   | E |
|   |   |   |   | 24 J | O | H | N |   |   |   |   | R |   |   |   |   | R |   | N |
|   |   |   |   |   |   |   | T |   | 25 S | O | H | O |   |   |   |   | E |   |
|   |   |   |   |   |   |   |   |   |   |   |   | R |   | 26 G | R | E | E | N |

**Across**
1. Combination of good and evil
4. Hours Dr. Jekyll could go before changing to Mr. Hyde
5. Messrs.____:wholesale chemists
6. Pounds Mr. Hyde gave the family
10. Dr. Jekyll's nickname
11. Dr. Lanyon received the letter on this date
15. # of years Dr. Lanyon had not seen Dr. Jekyll
17. Sir Danvers Carew was a member of _____.
20. First color of the liquid
22. ____or ten: trampled girl's age
24. Mr. Utterson's middle name
25. Location of Mr. Hyde's house
26. Third color of the liquid/cheque book color

**Down**
2. Mr. Hyde's first name
3. Setting of novel
4. Mr. Utterson and Mr. Enfield's walking day
5. Witnessed the murder
7. Pure evil
8. ____Park: Dr. Jekyll involuntarily changed to Mr. Hyde here
9. First name of murdered man
10. Dr. Jekyll's first name
12. Dr. Jekyll and Mr. Hyde felt this for each other
13. Dr. Lanyon held it for Dr. Jekyll
14. Pounds for which the cheque was written
16. Inspector
17. Dr. Jekyll's servant
18. Time of murder/time the messenger came
19. Caused the change from Jekyll to Hyde
21. Dr. Lanyon felt this after his discovery
23. AM time when girl was trampled

# Dr. Jekyll & Mr. Hyde Crossword 4

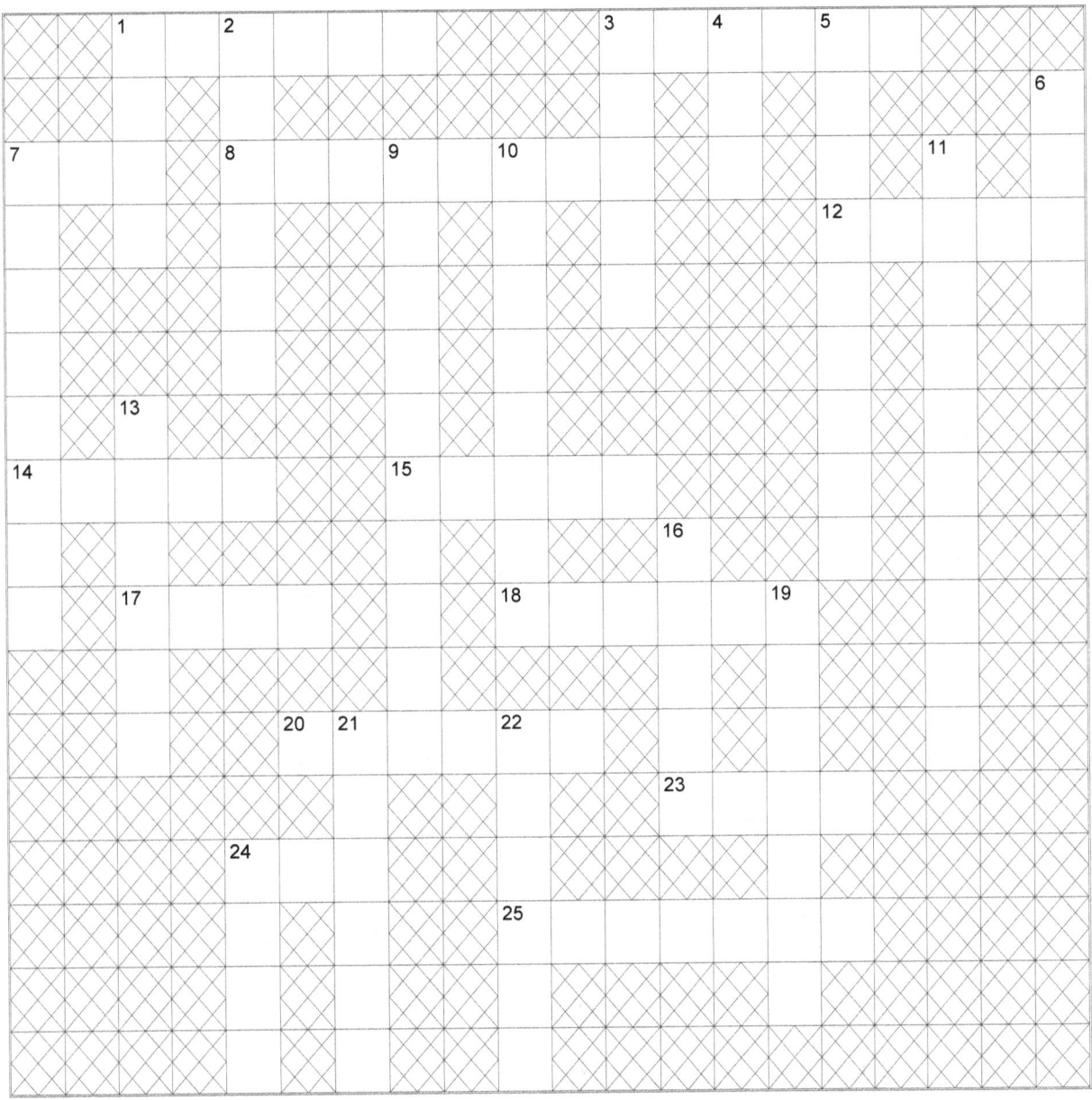

**Across**
1. Dr. Lanyon's first name
3. Dr. Jekyll and Mr. Hyde felt this for each other
7. First color of the liquid
8. Inspector
12. Dr. Lanyon received the letter on this date
14. AM time when girl was trampled
15. ____or ten: trampled girl's age
17. Mr. Utterson had Dr. Jekyll's
18. Dr. Lanyon felt this after his discovery
20. Combination of good and evil
23. Location of Mr. Hyde's house
24. Messrs.____:wholesale chemists
25. First name of murdered man

**Down**
1. Pure evil
2. Mr. Utterson and Mr. Enfield's walking day
3. Dr. Jekyll's first name
4. # of years Dr. Lanyon had not seen Dr. Jekyll
5. Dr. Jekyll's accent
6. Mr. Utterson's middle name
7. ____Park: Dr. Jekyll involuntarily changed to Mr. Hyde here
9. Mr. Utterson took it from the fire
10. Time of murder/time the messenger came
11. Pounds Mr. Hyde gave the family
13. Dr. Lanyon held it for Dr. Jekyll
16. Caused the change from Jekyll to Hyde
19. Mr. Enfield's first name
21. Mr. Hyde's first name
22. Setting of novel
24. Witnessed the murder

# Dr. Jekyll & Mr. Hyde Crossword 4 Answer Key

|   |   | 1 H | 2 S | T | I | E |   | 3 H | 4 A | 5 T | R | E | D |   |
|---|---|---|---|---|---|---|---|---|---|---|---|---|---|---|
|   |   | Y |   U |   |   |   |   | E | E | D |   |   |   | 6 J |
| 7 R | E | D | 8 N | E | 9 W | 10 C | O | M | E | N |   | N |   | 11 O | O |
| E |   | E | E |   | D |   H |   | I |   R |   |   | 12 N | I | N | T | H |
| G |   |   | A |   |   |   E |   | D |   Y |   |   | B |   | E |   | N |
| E |   |   | Y |   |   |   Q |   | N |   |   |   | U |   | H |   |   |
| N |   | 13 D |   |   |   U |   | I |   |   |   | R |   | U |   |   |
| 14 T | H | R | E | E |   | 15 E | I | G | H | T |   |   | G |   | N |   |
| ' |   |   | A |   |   |   |   B |   | H |   | 16 D |   | H |   | D |   |
| S |   | 17 W | I | L | L |   |   O |   | 18 T | E | R | R | O | 19 R |   | R |
|   |   | E |   |   |   |   O |   |   |   |   | U |   | I |   | E |
|   |   | R |   | 20 J | 21 E | K | Y | 22 L | L |   | G |   | C |   | D |
|   |   |   |   |   D |   |   |   |   O |   | 23 S | O | H | O |   |
|   |   |   | 24 M | A | W |   |   | N |   |   |   |   | A |   |
|   |   |   | A |   | A |   | 25 D | A | N | V | E | R | S |   |
|   |   |   | I |   | R |   | O |   |   |   | D |   |   |
|   |   |   | D |   | D |   | N |   |   |   |   |   |   |

**Across**
1. Dr. Lanyon's first name
3. Dr. Jekyll and Mr. Hyde felt this for each other
7. First color of the liquid
8. Inspector
12. Dr. Lanyon received the letter on this date
14. AM time when girl was trampled
15. ____or ten: trampled girl's age
17. Mr. Utterson had Dr. Jekyll's
18. Dr. Lanyon felt this after his discovery
20. Combination of good and evil
23. Location of Mr. Hyde's house
24. Messrs.____:wholesale chemists
25. First name of murdered man

**Down**
1. Pure evil
2. Mr. Utterson and Mr. Enfield's walking day
3. Dr. Jekyll's first name
4. # of years Dr. Lanyon had not seen Dr. Jekyll
5. Dr. Jekyll's accent
6. Mr. Utterson's middle name
7. ____Park: Dr. Jekyll involuntarily changed to Mr. Hyde here
9. Mr. Utterson took it from the fire
10. Time of murder/time the messenger came
11. Pounds Mr. Hyde gave the family
13. Dr. Lanyon held it for Dr. Jekyll
16. Caused the change from Jekyll to Hyde
19. Mr. Enfield's first name
21. Mr. Hyde's first name
22. Setting of novel
24. Witnessed the murder

Dr. Jekyll & Mr. Hyde

| PORTLAND | WALKS | PARLIAMENT | MAID | UTTERSON |
|---|---|---|---|---|
| GAIETY | DRAWER | BLACK MAIL | RED | EDWARD |
| GALLOWS | LONDON | FREE SPACE | TEN | HYDE |
| CAVENDISH | DRUGS | HARRY | THREE | SOHO |
| GUEST | WILL | MIDNIGHT | JOHN | HASTIE |

Dr. Jekyll & Mr. Hyde

| SCOTLAND | SIX | BRADSHAW | RICHARD | REGENT'S |
|---|---|---|---|---|
| EIGHT | MAW | EDINBURGH | POOLE | HATRED |
| CANE | GABRIEL | FREE SPACE | ENFIELD | HENRY |
| GREEN | NINTH | NINETY | LANYON | SUNDAY |
| JEKYLL | DANVERS | CHEQUE BOOK | TERROR | PURPLE |

Dr. Jekyll & Mr. Hyde

| HOUSEKEEPER | MIDNIGHT | POOLE | TEN | JOHN |
|---|---|---|---|---|
| DRAWER | HATRED | SCOTLAND | EIGHT | GUEST |
| JEKYLL | GAIETY | FREE SPACE | NINETY | DANVERS |
| NINTH | ENFIELD | CHEQUE BOOK | BLACK MAIL | REGENT'S |
| ONE HUNDRED | HASTIE | GREEN | THREE | GALLOWS |

Dr. Jekyll & Mr. Hyde

| CANE | MAW | WILL | PORTLAND | RICHARD |
|---|---|---|---|---|
| SUNDAY | HARRY | LANYON | JANUARY | DRUGS |
| LONDON | TERROR | FREE SPACE | EDWARD | RED |
| UTTERSON | NEWCOMEN | MAID | GABRIEL | BRADSHAW |
| PURPLE | CAVENDISH | DENMAN | EDINBURGH | HENRY |

Dr. Jekyll & Mr. Hyde

| PORTLAND | ONE HUNDRED | WALKS | HOUSEKEEPER | EDWARD |
|---|---|---|---|---|
| NINETY | REGENT'S | DRUGS | MAID | DRAWER |
| MAW | MIDNIGHT | FREE SPACE | TERROR | HASTIE |
| SIX | HARRY | LANYON | SCOTLAND | UTTERSON |
| NEWCOMEN | HATRED | WILL | SOHO | CAVENDISH |

Dr. Jekyll & Mr. Hyde

| GAIETY | POOLE | GUEST | RICHARD | DENMAN |
|---|---|---|---|---|
| NINTH | THREE | HYDE | GALLOWS | BLACK MAIL |
| PURPLE | GABRIEL | FREE SPACE | LONDON | JANUARY |
| BRADSHAW | PARLIAMENT | RED | SUNDAY | HENRY |
| GREEN | EIGHT | JOHN | CHEQUE BOOK | TEN |

Dr. Jekyll & Mr. Hyde

| LONDON | PURPLE | HASTIE | TERROR | NEWCOMEN |
|---|---|---|---|---|
| HYDE | GUEST | DRUGS | DENMAN | NINETY |
| SOHO | SCOTLAND | FREE SPACE | TEN | EIGHT |
| GREEN | RICHARD | UTTERSON | NINTH | REGENT'S |
| ONE HUNDRED | MAW | GALLOWS | GAIETY | GABRIEL |

Dr. Jekyll & Mr. Hyde

| DANVERS | JOHN | ENFIELD | EDWARD | SIX |
|---|---|---|---|---|
| DRAWER | JANUARY | MIDNIGHT | EDINBURGH | BLACK MAIL |
| LANYON | BRADSHAW | FREE SPACE | CAVENDISH | HENRY |
| HARRY | RED | THREE | PARLIAMENT | SUNDAY |
| MAID | CANE | POOLE | WILL | WALKS |

Dr. Jekyll & Mr. Hyde

| WALKS | HATRED | PORTLAND | SUNDAY | JOHN |
|---|---|---|---|---|
| TERROR | LANYON | GABRIEL | CANE | CHEQUE BOOK |
| DENMAN | BLACK MAIL | FREE SPACE | RICHARD | TEN |
| EIGHT | DRUGS | RED | DANVERS | JANUARY |
| THREE | LONDON | EDWARD | HASTIE | POOLE |

Dr. Jekyll & Mr. Hyde

| SOHO | PARLIAMENT | SIX | REGENT'S | NINTH |
|---|---|---|---|---|
| CAVENDISH | EDINBURGH | MIDNIGHT | NEWCOMEN | ENFIELD |
| HARRY | GALLOWS | FREE SPACE | UTTERSON | PURPLE |
| GAIETY | JEKYLL | GUEST | WILL | DRAWER |
| BRADSHAW | HOUSEKEEPER | MAW | MAID | SCOTLAND |

Dr. Jekyll & Mr. Hyde

| EIGHT | ONE HUNDRED | NINTH | HYDE | EDINBURGH |
|---|---|---|---|---|
| DRUGS | HENRY | MAW | WILL | JANUARY |
| UTTERSON | MIDNIGHT | FREE SPACE | PORTLAND | ENFIELD |
| CHEQUE BOOK | CANE | DRAWER | SIX | REGENT'S |
| MAID | LANYON | RICHARD | HASTIE | PURPLE |

Dr. Jekyll & Mr. Hyde

| SUNDAY | THREE | HOUSEKEEPER | GABRIEL | LONDON |
|---|---|---|---|---|
| HARRY | NEWCOMEN | POOLE | RED | BLACK MAIL |
| SOHO | DANVERS | FREE SPACE | GAIETY | PARLIAMENT |
| HATRED | BRADSHAW | CAVENDISH | JEKYLL | SCOTLAND |
| GUEST | DENMAN | EDWARD | NINETY | GREEN |

Dr. Jekyll & Mr. Hyde

| GUEST | CAVENDISH | SCOTLAND | JOHN | SUNDAY |
|---|---|---|---|---|
| PURPLE | JANUARY | REGENT'S | HATRED | PARLIAMENT |
| MIDNIGHT | PORTLAND | FREE SPACE | DANVERS | JEKYLL |
| EIGHT | GABRIEL | MAW | WALKS | HOUSEKEEPER |
| TEN | HENRY | LANYON | LONDON | NINTH |

Dr. Jekyll & Mr. Hyde

| HARRY | WILL | GAIETY | DRUGS | GALLOWS |
|---|---|---|---|---|
| EDINBURGH | SIX | SOHO | HASTIE | RICHARD |
| ONE HUNDRED | CHEQUE BOOK | FREE SPACE | BRADSHAW | RED |
| POOLE | EDWARD | THREE | BLACK MAIL | NINETY |
| GREEN | NEWCOMEN | TERROR | DENMAN | MAID |

Dr. Jekyll & Mr. Hyde

| GAIETY | HOUSEKEEPER | BLACK MAIL | DRAWER | HENRY |
|---|---|---|---|---|
| GUEST | ONE HUNDRED | PORTLAND | SUNDAY | JOHN |
| GABRIEL | EDWARD | FREE SPACE | DANVERS | TERROR |
| WILL | TEN | GALLOWS | RICHARD | HATRED |
| HYDE | SCOTLAND | JEKYLL | LONDON | PARLIAMENT |

Dr. Jekyll & Mr. Hyde

| CANE | THREE | HASTIE | NEWCOMEN | MAID |
|---|---|---|---|---|
| ENFIELD | WALKS | EDINBURGH | EIGHT | CAVENDISH |
| NINTH | REGENT'S | FREE SPACE | MIDNIGHT | CHEQUE BOOK |
| LANYON | BRADSHAW | PURPLE | POOLE | GREEN |
| HARRY | UTTERSON | JANUARY | DENMAN | RED |

Dr. Jekyll & Mr. Hyde

| MAID | GALLOWS | RICHARD | WILL | BRADSHAW |
|---|---|---|---|---|
| HATRED | GABRIEL | DRUGS | WALKS | PARLIAMENT |
| NINTH | GUEST | FREE SPACE | CHEQUE BOOK | DENMAN |
| JOHN | JANUARY | TERROR | HOUSEKEEPER | LANYON |
| CANE | TEN | PURPLE | MAW | BLACK MAIL |

Dr. Jekyll & Mr. Hyde

| SIX | MIDNIGHT | CAVENDISH | EDINBURGH | HARRY |
|---|---|---|---|---|
| PORTLAND | GAIETY | HYDE | GREEN | HENRY |
| ONE HUNDRED | POOLE | FREE SPACE | LONDON | NINETY |
| RED | NEWCOMEN | DRAWER | DANVERS | EIGHT |
| SOHO | JEKYLL | THREE | ENFIELD | SCOTLAND |

Dr. Jekyll & Mr. Hyde

| | | | | |
|---|---|---|---|---|
| UTTERSON | ENFIELD | LONDON | CANE | BLACK MAIL |
| GREEN | LANYON | PARLIAMENT | GUEST | TEN |
| HATRED | RED | FREE SPACE | NINETY | GALLOWS |
| DRAWER | DENMAN | HOUSEKEEPER | JEKYLL | MAW |
| EDWARD | TERROR | WILL | CAVENDISH | NEWCOMEN |

Dr. Jekyll & Mr. Hyde

| | | | | |
|---|---|---|---|---|
| JOHN | HENRY | SIX | DRUGS | SUNDAY |
| BRADSHAW | GAIETY | SOHO | EIGHT | HYDE |
| DANVERS | JANUARY | FREE SPACE | GABRIEL | EDINBURGH |
| ONE HUNDRED | HARRY | REGENT'S | SCOTLAND | WALKS |
| NINTH | CHEQUE BOOK | PURPLE | MAID | HASTIE |

Dr. Jekyll & Mr. Hyde

| DRAWER | GREEN | MIDNIGHT | SIX | ONE HUNDRED |
|---|---|---|---|---|
| GAIETY | DRUGS | LONDON | PURPLE | HASTIE |
| DANVERS | WILL | FREE SPACE | GALLOWS | CHEQUE BOOK |
| DENMAN | RICHARD | TERROR | WALKS | JEKYLL |
| SUNDAY | BLACK MAIL | GUEST | GABRIEL | PARLIAMENT |

Dr. Jekyll & Mr. Hyde

| MAID | HENRY | THREE | TEN | NINTH |
|---|---|---|---|---|
| RED | CANE | SCOTLAND | CAVENDISH | ENFIELD |
| JANUARY | HARRY | FREE SPACE | HYDE | JOHN |
| NEWCOMEN | MAW | POOLE | HOUSEKEEPER | NINETY |
| SOHO | EIGHT | REGENT'S | HATRED | BRADSHAW |

Dr. Jekyll & Mr. Hyde

| SUNDAY | POOLE | DRAWER | DENMAN | BLACK MAIL |
|---|---|---|---|---|
| RICHARD | RED | HASTIE | LONDON | PURPLE |
| DANVERS | HATRED | FREE SPACE | EDINBURGH | GAIETY |
| JEKYLL | DRUGS | TERROR | HYDE | JANUARY |
| MIDNIGHT | BRADSHAW | ONE HUNDRED | CHEQUE BOOK | NEWCOMEN |

Dr. Jekyll & Mr. Hyde

| TEN | HOUSEKEEPER | CAVENDISH | SCOTLAND | WILL |
|---|---|---|---|---|
| REGENT'S | EDWARD | ENFIELD | MAID | CANE |
| JOHN | UTTERSON | FREE SPACE | GABRIEL | WALKS |
| MAW | LANYON | HENRY | NINETY | GUEST |
| SOHO | PARLIAMENT | NINTH | SIX | PORTLAND |

Dr. Jekyll & Mr. Hyde

| GUEST | WILL | MAW | NINTH | REGENT'S |
|---|---|---|---|---|
| CANE | JANUARY | PURPLE | MIDNIGHT | DRUGS |
| THREE | PORTLAND | FREE SPACE | MAID | JEKYLL |
| GALLOWS | EDINBURGH | GAIETY | SCOTLAND | TERROR |
| HATRED | JOHN | SIX | UTTERSON | NEWCOMEN |

Dr. Jekyll & Mr. Hyde

| TEN | BRADSHAW | BLACK MAIL | WALKS | DANVERS |
|---|---|---|---|---|
| GREEN | GABRIEL | HARRY | DENMAN | HENRY |
| POOLE | SOHO | FREE SPACE | NINETY | EIGHT |
| HOUSEKEEPER | PARLIAMENT | LANYON | DRAWER | HASTIE |
| HYDE | CHEQUE BOOK | CAVENDISH | LONDON | ONE HUNDRED |

Dr. Jekyll & Mr. Hyde

| EDWARD | TERROR | POOLE | ENFIELD | JANUARY |
|---|---|---|---|---|
| EDINBURGH | HARRY | SOHO | HOUSEKEEPER | BLACK MAIL |
| DANVERS | HYDE | FREE SPACE | JOHN | NEWCOMEN |
| SUNDAY | NINTH | PURPLE | CANE | TEN |
| NINETY | DENMAN | PARLIAMENT | PORTLAND | REGENT'S |

Dr. Jekyll & Mr. Hyde

| HASTIE | CHEQUE BOOK | WALKS | GAIETY | RICHARD |
|---|---|---|---|---|
| MAW | MIDNIGHT | GABRIEL | EIGHT | DRUGS |
| GREEN | GUEST | FREE SPACE | ONE HUNDRED | LANYON |
| UTTERSON | HENRY | DRAWER | JEKYLL | WILL |
| MAID | THREE | CAVENDISH | GALLOWS | BRADSHAW |

Dr. Jekyll & Mr. Hyde

| GABRIEL | RICHARD | ONE HUNDRED | SIX | DENMAN |
|---|---|---|---|---|
| DANVERS | TERROR | CHEQUE BOOK | DRUGS | CANE |
| GREEN | BRADSHAW | FREE SPACE | ENFIELD | REGENT'S |
| HOUSEKEEPER | HARRY | HATRED | MAW | EIGHT |
| DRAWER | JANUARY | NEWCOMEN | GAIETY | GUEST |

Dr. Jekyll & Mr. Hyde

| MIDNIGHT | JOHN | CAVENDISH | PURPLE | TEN |
|---|---|---|---|---|
| NINETY | EDWARD | RED | EDINBURGH | POOLE |
| SUNDAY | JEKYLL | FREE SPACE | PARLIAMENT | LONDON |
| WILL | LANYON | HYDE | HASTIE | UTTERSON |
| SOHO | BLACK MAIL | MAID | SCOTLAND | NINTH |

Dr. Jekyll & Mr. Hyde

| CANE | SCOTLAND | MAW | EDWARD | NEWCOMEN |
|---|---|---|---|---|
| WALKS | LANYON | DANVERS | SIX | HASTIE |
| WILL | EIGHT | FREE SPACE | DRAWER | BRADSHAW |
| LONDON | HENRY | UTTERSON | HARRY | HATRED |
| JOHN | DENMAN | ENFIELD | TEN | RED |

Dr. Jekyll & Mr. Hyde

| RICHARD | GUEST | TERROR | CAVENDISH | JEKYLL |
|---|---|---|---|---|
| NINTH | MIDNIGHT | PURPLE | REGENT'S | PORTLAND |
| GREEN | GALLOWS | FREE SPACE | JANUARY | EDINBURGH |
| SOHO | ONE HUNDRED | GABRIEL | DRUGS | BLACK MAIL |
| HYDE | POOLE | PARLIAMENT | THREE | CHEQUE BOOK |

# Dr. Jekyll & Mr. Hyde Vocabulary Word List

| No. | Word | Clue/Definition |
|---|---|---|
| 1. | ABJECT | Wretched; lacking pride |
| 2. | ACCOSTED | Spoke to first |
| 3. | AUSTERE | Strict; stern |
| 4. | AVERSIONS | Firm dislike |
| 5. | CALAMITY | Disaster |
| 6. | CAPACIOUS | Large |
| 7. | CONDONED | Overlooked; forgiven |
| 8. | CONFLAGRATION | A great fire |
| 9. | DETESTABLE | Hateful; nasty |
| 10. | DISCONSOLATE | Sad |
| 11. | DISINTERRED | Dug up |
| 12. | EFFICACY | Power to produce the desired effect |
| 13. | EMINENTLY | Outstanding |
| 14. | ENDOWED | Provided |
| 15. | ENIGMAS | Puzzles |
| 16. | EXORBITANT | Excessive |
| 17. | GAUNT | Lean and angler |
| 18. | IMPERIOUS | Domineering; arrogant |
| 19. | INCIPIENT | Beginning; in an early stage |
| 20. | INCOHERENCY | Unable to express one's thoughts clearly |
| 21. | INCONGRUOUS | Absurd; incompatible |
| 22. | INIQUITY | Wickedness; injustice |
| 23. | INSENSATE | Without feeling |
| 24. | INVETERATELY | Deep rooted; habitually |
| 25. | LAMENTATION | Grieving; expressing sorrow |
| 26. | MIEN | Behavior; bearing |
| 27. | MULTIFARIOUS | Varied: greatly diversified |
| 28. | ODIOUS | Hateful |
| 29. | PECUNIARY | Relating to money |
| 30. | PERENNIAL | Continuing: recurring |
| 31. | PERPLEXITY | Confusion; puzzlement |
| 32. | PROTEGE | A person under the support of a patron |
| 33. | REPOSE | To place trust in |
| 34. | REPROVE | Rebuke; scold |
| 35. | RUMINATED | Pondered; reflected over and over |
| 36. | SCRUTINY | Close examination |
| 37. | SEDULOUSLY | Diligently |
| 38. | SOMBRE | Gloom; depressing |
| 39. | UNOBTRUSIVE | Not noticeable |
| 40. | VOLATILE | Evaporating rapidly |

Dr. Jekyll & Mr. Hyde Vocabulary Fill In The Blank 1

_____  1. A person under the support of a patron

_____  2. Excessive

_____  3. Strict; stern

_____  4. Not noticeable

_____  5. Grieving; expressing sorrow

_____  6. Wretched; lacking pride

_____  7. Spoke to first

_____  8. Unable to express one's thoughts clearly

_____  9. Close examination

_____  10. To place trust in

_____  11. Outstanding

_____  12. Behavior; bearing

_____  13. Hateful

_____  14. Confusion; puzzlement

_____  15. Overlooked; forgiven

_____  16. Large

_____  17. Puzzles

_____  18. Varied: greatly diversified

_____  19. Dug up

_____  20. Beginning; in an early stage

Dr. Jekyll & Mr. Hyde Vocabulary Fill In The Blank 1 Answer Key

| | |
|---|---|
| PROTEGE | 1. A person under the support of a patron |
| EXORBITANT | 2. Excessive |
| AUSTERE | 3. Strict; stern |
| UNOBTRUSIVE | 4. Not noticeable |
| LAMENTATION | 5. Grieving; expressing sorrow |
| ABJECT | 6. Wretched; lacking pride |
| ACCOSTED | 7. Spoke to first |
| INCOHERENCY | 8. Unable to express one's thoughts clearly |
| SCRUTINY | 9. Close examination |
| REPOSE | 10. To place trust in |
| EMINENTLY | 11. Outstanding |
| MIEN | 12. Behavior; bearing |
| ODIOUS | 13. Hateful |
| PERPLEXITY | 14. Confusion; puzzlement |
| CONDONED | 15. Overlooked; forgiven |
| CAPACIOUS | 16. Large |
| ENIGMAS | 17. Puzzles |
| MULTIFARIOUS | 18. Varied: greatly diversified |
| DISINTERRED | 19. Dug up |
| INCIPIENT | 20. Beginning; in an early stage |

Dr. Jekyll & Mr. Hyde Vocabulary Fill In The Blank 2

_____  1. Hateful; nasty

_____  2. Spoke to first

_____  3. Not noticeable

_____  4. A person under the support of a patron

_____  5. Puzzles

_____  6. Excessive

_____  7. Domineering; arrogant

_____  8. Continuing: recurring

_____  9. Gloom; depressing

_____  10. Grieving; expressing sorrow

_____  11. Absurd; incompatible

_____  12. Outstanding

_____  13. Wickedness; injustice

_____  14. Lean and angler

_____  15. Overlooked; forgiven

_____  16. Deep rooted; habitually

_____  17. Beginning; in an early stage

_____  18. Wretched; lacking pride

_____  19. A great fire

_____  20. Relating to money

# Dr. Jekyll & Mr. Hyde Vocabulary Fill In The Blank 2 Answer Key

| | |
|---|---|
| DETESTABLE | 1. Hateful; nasty |
| ACCOSTED | 2. Spoke to first |
| UNOBTRUSIVE | 3. Not noticeable |
| PROTEGE | 4. A person under the support of a patron |
| ENIGMAS | 5. Puzzles |
| EXORBITANT | 6. Excessive |
| IMPERIOUS | 7. Domineering; arrogant |
| PERENNIAL | 8. Continuing: recurring |
| SOMBRE | 9. Gloom; depressing |
| LAMENTATION | 10. Grieving; expressing sorrow |
| INCONGRUOUS | 11. Absurd; incompatible |
| EMINENTLY | 12. Outstanding |
| INIQUITY | 13. Wickedness; injustice |
| GAUNT | 14. Lean and angler |
| CONDONED | 15. Overlooked; forgiven |
| INVETERATELY | 16. Deep rooted; habitually |
| INCIPIENT | 17. Beginning; in an early stage |
| ABJECT | 18. Wretched; lacking pride |
| CONFLAGRATION | 19. A great fire |
| PECUNIARY | 20. Relating to money |

# Dr. Jekyll & Mr. Hyde Vocabulary Fill In The Blank 3

_____   1. Wickedness; injustice

_____   2. Domineering; arrogant

_____   3. Power to produce the desired effect

_____   4. Spoke to first

_____   5. Provided

_____   6. Continuing: recurring

_____   7. Pondered; reflected over and over

_____   8. Outstanding

_____   9. Hateful; nasty

_____   10. Without feeling

_____   11. Gloom; depressing

_____   12. Relating to money

_____   13. Hateful

_____   14. Dug up

_____   15. Sad

_____   16. Disaster

_____   17. Firm dislike

_____   18. To place trust in

_____   19. Lean and angler

_____   20. Overlooked; forgiven

Dr. Jekyll & Mr. Hyde Vocabulary Fill In The Blank 3 Answer Key

|  |  |
|---|---|
| INIQUITY | 1. Wickedness; injustice |
| IMPERIOUS | 2. Domineering; arrogant |
| EFFICACY | 3. Power to produce the desired effect |
| ACCOSTED | 4. Spoke to first |
| ENDOWED | 5. Provided |
| PERENNIAL | 6. Continuing: recurring |
| RUMINATED | 7. Pondered; reflected over and over |
| EMINENTLY | 8. Outstanding |
| DETESTABLE | 9. Hateful; nasty |
| INSENSATE | 10. Without feeling |
| SOMBRE | 11. Gloom; depressing |
| PECUNIARY | 12. Relating to money |
| ODIOUS | 13. Hateful |
| DISINTERRED | 14. Dug up |
| DISCONSOLATE | 15. Sad |
| CALAMITY | 16. Disaster |
| AVERSIONS | 17. Firm dislike |
| REPOSE | 18. To place trust in |
| GAUNT | 19. Lean and angler |
| CONDONED | 20. Overlooked; forgiven |

Dr. Jekyll & Mr. Hyde Vocabulary Fill In The Blank 4

_____  1. A great fire
_____  2. Continuing: recurring
_____  3. Firm dislike
_____  4. Not noticeable
_____  5. Lean and angler
_____  6. Power to produce the desired effect
_____  7. Strict; stern
_____  8. Wickedness; injustice
_____  9. Hateful; nasty
_____  10. Large
_____  11. Absurd; incompatible
_____  12. A person under the support of a patron
_____  13. Disaster
_____  14. Excessive
_____  15. Overlooked; forgiven
_____  16. Domineering; arrogant
_____  17. Varied: greatly diversified
_____  18. Grieving; expressing sorrow
_____  19. Puzzles
_____  20. Pondered; reflected over and over

Dr. Jekyll & Mr. Hyde Vocabulary Fill In The Blank 4 Answer Key

| | |
|---|---|
| CONFLAGRATION | 1. A great fire |
| PERENNIAL | 2. Continuing: recurring |
| AVERSIONS | 3. Firm dislike |
| UNOBTRUSIVE | 4. Not noticeable |
| GAUNT | 5. Lean and angler |
| EFFICACY | 6. Power to produce the desired effect |
| AUSTERE | 7. Strict; stern |
| INIQUITY | 8. Wickedness; injustice |
| DETESTABLE | 9. Hateful; nasty |
| CAPACIOUS | 10. Large |
| INCONGRUOUS | 11. Absurd; incompatible |
| PROTEGE | 12. A person under the support of a patron |
| CALAMITY | 13. Disaster |
| EXORBITANT | 14. Excessive |
| CONDONED | 15. Overlooked; forgiven |
| IMPERIOUS | 16. Domineering; arrogant |
| MULTIFARIOUS | 17. Varied: greatly diversified |
| LAMENTATION | 18. Grieving; expressing sorrow |
| ENIGMAS | 19. Puzzles |
| RUMINATED | 20. Pondered; reflected over and over |

Dr. Jekyll & Mr. Hyde Vocabulary Matching 1

___ 1. INCOHERENCY        A. Hateful
___ 2. CALAMITY           B. Gloom; depressing
___ 3. INVETERATELY       C. Outstanding
___ 4. PECUNIARY          D. Not noticeable
___ 5. ENIGMAS            E. Wickedness; injustice
___ 6. GAUNT              F. A great fire
___ 7. ODIOUS             G. A person under the support of a patron
___ 8. REPROVE            H. Hateful; nasty
___ 9. SCRUTINY           I. Absurd; incompatible
___10. AUSTERE            J. Grieving; expressing sorrow
___11. LAMENTATION        K. Without feeling
___12. SOMBRE             L. Deep rooted; habitually
___13. PERENNIAL          M. Excessive
___14. EXORBITANT         N. Evaporating rapidly
___15. INCONGRUOUS        O. Strict; stern
___16. ACCOSTED           P. Continuing: recurring
___17. INIQUITY           Q. Relating to money
___18. INSENSATE          R. Disaster
___19. CONFLAGRATION      S. Puzzles
___20. VOLATILE           T. Close examination
___21. EMINENTLY          U. Rebuke; scold
___22. DISINTERRED        V. Unable to express one's thoughts clearly
___23. PROTEGE            W. Spoke to first
___24. DETESTABLE         X. Lean and angler
___25. UNOBTRUSIVE        Y. Dug up

Dr. Jekyll & Mr. Hyde Vocabulary Matching 1 Answer Key

V - 1. INCOHERENCY	A. Hateful
R - 2. CALAMITY	B. Gloom; depressing
L - 3. INVETERATELY	C. Outstanding
Q - 4. PECUNIARY	D. Not noticeable
S - 5. ENIGMAS	E. Wickedness; injustice
X - 6. GAUNT	F. A great fire
A - 7. ODIOUS	G. A person under the support of a patron
U - 8. REPROVE	H. Hateful; nasty
T - 9. SCRUTINY	I. Absurd; incompatible
O -10. AUSTERE	J. Grieving; expressing sorrow
J -11. LAMENTATION	K. Without feeling
B -12. SOMBRE	L. Deep rooted; habitually
P -13. PERENNIAL	M. Excessive
M -14. EXORBITANT	N. Evaporating rapidly
I -15. INCONGRUOUS	O. Strict; stern
W -16. ACCOSTED	P. Continuing: recurring
E -17. INIQUITY	Q. Relating to money
K -18. INSENSATE	R. Disaster
F -19. CONFLAGRATION	S. Puzzles
N -20. VOLATILE	T. Close examination
C -21. EMINENTLY	U. Rebuke; scold
Y -22. DISINTERRED	V. Unable to express one's thoughts clearly
G -23. PROTEGE	W. Spoke to first
H -24. DETESTABLE	X. Lean and angler
D -25. UNOBTRUSIVE	Y. Dug up

Dr. Jekyll & Mr. Hyde Vocabulary Matching 2

___ 1. REPROVE             A. Varied: greatly diversified
___ 2. SCRUTINY            B. Disaster
___ 3. EXORBITANT          C. Pondered; reflected over and over
___ 4. IMPERIOUS           D. Grieving; expressing sorrow
___ 5. DETESTABLE          E. Dug up
___ 6. DISCONSOLATE        F. Rebuke; scold
___ 7. VOLATILE            G. Hateful; nasty
___ 8. CONFLAGRATION       H. Excessive
___ 9. RUMINATED           I. Beginning; in an early stage
___10. GAUNT               J. Sad
___11. UNOBTRUSIVE         K. Hateful
___12. ABJECT              L. Domineering; arrogant
___13. INIQUITY            M. Close examination
___14. LAMENTATION         N. Puzzles
___15. AUSTERE             O. A great fire
___16. EMINENTLY           P. Outstanding
___17. DISINTERRED         Q. Wretched; lacking pride
___18. MULTIFARIOUS        R. Lean and angler
___19. ODIOUS              S. Strict; stern
___20. CALAMITY            T. Deep rooted; habitually
___21. ENIGMAS             U. Spoke to first
___22. INVETERATELY        V. Evaporating rapidly
___23. REPOSE              W. Wickedness; injustice
___24. INCIPIENT           X. To place trust in
___25. ACCOSTED            Y. Not noticeable

Dr. Jekyll & Mr. Hyde Vocabulary Matching 2 Answer Key

| | | |
|---|---|---|
| F - 1. | REPROVE | A. Varied: greatly diversified |
| M - 2. | SCRUTINY | B. Disaster |
| H - 3. | EXORBITANT | C. Pondered; reflected over and over |
| L - 4. | IMPERIOUS | D. Grieving; expressing sorrow |
| G - 5. | DETESTABLE | E. Dug up |
| J - 6. | DISCONSOLATE | F. Rebuke; scold |
| V - 7. | VOLATILE | G. Hateful; nasty |
| O - 8. | CONFLAGRATION | H. Excessive |
| C - 9. | RUMINATED | I. Beginning; in an early stage |
| R -10. | GAUNT | J. Sad |
| Y -11. | UNOBTRUSIVE | K. Hateful |
| Q -12. | ABJECT | L. Domineering; arrogant |
| W -13. | INIQUITY | M. Close examination |
| D -14. | LAMENTATION | N. Puzzles |
| S -15. | AUSTERE | O. A great fire |
| P -16. | EMINENTLY | P. Outstanding |
| E -17. | DISINTERRED | Q. Wretched; lacking pride |
| A -18. | MULTIFARIOUS | R. Lean and angler |
| K -19. | ODIOUS | S. Strict; stern |
| B -20. | CALAMITY | T. Deep rooted; habitually |
| N -21. | ENIGMAS | U. Spoke to first |
| T -22. | INVETERATELY | V. Evaporating rapidly |
| X -23. | REPOSE | W. Wickedness; injustice |
| I - 24. | INCIPIENT | X. To place trust in |
| U -25. | ACCOSTED | Y. Not noticeable |

Dr. Jekyll & Mr. Hyde Vocabulary Matching 3

___ 1. SCRUTINY           A. Provided
___ 2. LAMENTATION         B. Power to produce the desired effect
___ 3. PERPLEXITY          C. Not noticeable
___ 4. PECUNIARY           D. Firm dislike
___ 5. ENIGMAS             E. Dug up
___ 6. INSENSATE           F. Large
___ 7. EFFICACY            G. Spoke to first
___ 8. INVETERATELY        H. Grieving; expressing sorrow
___ 9. MULTIFARIOUS        I. Overlooked; forgiven
___10. ACCOSTED            J. Varied: greatly diversified
___11. AVERSIONS           K. Relating to money
___12. EXORBITANT          L. Without feeling
___13. GAUNT               M. Deep rooted; habitually
___14. ENDOWED             N. Domineering; arrogant
___15. CALAMITY            O. Strict; stern
___16. DISCONSOLATE        P. Excessive
___17. CAPACIOUS           Q. Disaster
___18. EMINENTLY           R. Sad
___19. REPROVE             S. Confusion; puzzlement
___20. IMPERIOUS           T. Lean and angler
___21. AUSTERE             U. Rebuke; scold
___22. DISINTERRED         V. Close examination
___23. UNOBTRUSIVE         W. Puzzles
___24. DETESTABLE          X. Outstanding
___25. CONDONED            Y. Hateful; nasty

Dr. Jekyll & Mr. Hyde Vocabulary Matching 3 Answer Key

| | | |
|---|---|---|
| V - 1. SCRUTINY | A. | Provided |
| H - 2. LAMENTATION | B. | Power to produce the desired effect |
| S - 3. PERPLEXITY | C. | Not noticeable |
| K - 4. PECUNIARY | D. | Firm dislike |
| W - 5. ENIGMAS | E. | Dug up |
| L - 6. INSENSATE | F. | Large |
| B - 7. EFFICACY | G. | Spoke to first |
| M - 8. INVETERATELY | H. | Grieving; expressing sorrow |
| J - 9. MULTIFARIOUS | I. | Overlooked; forgiven |
| G - 10. ACCOSTED | J. | Varied: greatly diversified |
| D - 11. AVERSIONS | K. | Relating to money |
| P - 12. EXORBITANT | L. | Without feeling |
| T - 13. GAUNT | M. | Deep rooted; habitually |
| A - 14. ENDOWED | N. | Domineering; arrogant |
| Q - 15. CALAMITY | O. | Strict; stern |
| R - 16. DISCONSOLATE | P. | Excessive |
| F - 17. CAPACIOUS | Q. | Disaster |
| X - 18. EMINENTLY | R. | Sad |
| U - 19. REPROVE | S. | Confusion; puzzlement |
| N - 20. IMPERIOUS | T. | Lean and angler |
| O - 21. AUSTERE | U. | Rebuke; scold |
| E - 22. DISINTERRED | V. | Close examination |
| C - 23. UNOBTRUSIVE | W. | Puzzles |
| Y - 24. DETESTABLE | X. | Outstanding |
| I - 25. CONDONED | Y. | Hateful; nasty |

Dr. Jekyll & Mr. Hyde Vocabulary Matching 4

___ 1. PERENNIAL         A. Grieving; expressing sorrow
___ 2. SCRUTINY          B. Firm dislike
___ 3. INCIPIENT         C. Spoke to first
___ 4. VOLATILE          D. Large
___ 5. INCONGRUOUS       E. Close examination
___ 6. INVETERATELY      F. Hateful; nasty
___ 7. INCOHERENCY       G. Wickedness; injustice
___ 8. AVERSIONS         H. Evaporating rapidly
___ 9. UNOBTRUSIVE       I. Pondered; reflected over and over
___10. INSENSATE         J. Puzzles
___11. GAUNT             K. Overlooked; forgiven
___12. ENIGMAS           L. Beginning; in an early stage
___13. SEDULOUSLY        M. Wretched; lacking pride
___14. CONDONED          N. Not noticeable
___15. LAMENTATION       O. Disaster
___16. ABJECT            P. Unable to express one's thoughts clearly
___17. RUMINATED         Q. Continuing: recurring
___18. DETESTABLE        R. Outstanding
___19. EMINENTLY         S. Absurd; incompatible
___20. CALAMITY          T. Gloom; depressing
___21. INIQUITY          U. Diligently
___22. CAPACIOUS         V. Strict; stern
___23. AUSTERE           W. Without feeling
___24. SOMBRE            X. Lean and angler
___25. ACCOSTED          Y. Deep rooted; habitually

Dr. Jekyll & Mr. Hyde Vocabulary Matching 4 Answer Key

| | | | |
|---|---|---|---|
| Q - 1. | PERENNIAL | A. | Grieving; expressing sorrow |
| E - 2. | SCRUTINY | B. | Firm dislike |
| L - 3. | INCIPIENT | C. | Spoke to first |
| H - 4. | VOLATILE | D. | Large |
| S - 5. | INCONGRUOUS | E. | Close examination |
| Y - 6. | INVETERATELY | F. | Hateful; nasty |
| P - 7. | INCOHERENCY | G. | Wickedness; injustice |
| B - 8. | AVERSIONS | H. | Evaporating rapidly |
| N - 9. | UNOBTRUSIVE | I. | Pondered; reflected over and over |
| W -10. | INSENSATE | J. | Puzzles |
| X -11. | GAUNT | K. | Overlooked; forgiven |
| J -12. | ENIGMAS | L. | Beginning; in an early stage |
| U -13. | SEDULOUSLY | M. | Wretched; lacking pride |
| K -14. | CONDONED | N. | Not noticeable |
| A -15. | LAMENTATION | O. | Disaster |
| M -16. | ABJECT | P. | Unable to express one's thoughts clearly |
| I -17. | RUMINATED | Q. | Continuing: recurring |
| F -18. | DETESTABLE | R. | Outstanding |
| R -19. | EMINENTLY | S. | Absurd; incompatible |
| O -20. | CALAMITY | T. | Gloom; depressing |
| G -21. | INIQUITY | U. | Diligently |
| D -22. | CAPACIOUS | V. | Strict; stern |
| V -23. | AUSTERE | W. | Without feeling |
| T -24. | SOMBRE | X. | Lean and angler |
| C -25. | ACCOSTED | Y. | Deep rooted; habitually |

Dr. Jekyll & Mr. Hyde Vocabulary Magic Squares 1

Match the definition with the vocabulary word. Put your answers in the magic squares below. When your answers are correct, all columns and rows will add to the same number.

A. VOLATILE
B. DETESTABLE
C. INSENSATE
D. UNOBTRUSIVE
E. PECUNIARY
F. GAUNT
G. ENIGMAS
H. REPROVE
I. DISINTERRED
J. CONFLAGRATION
K. INIQUITY
L. AUSTERE
M. SCRUTINY
N. INCIPIENT
O. DISCONSOLATE
P. ODIOUS

1. Hateful; nasty
2. Puzzles
3. Wickedness; injustice
4. Beginning; in an early stage
5. Close examination
6. Strict; stern
7. Rebuke; scold
8. Evaporating rapidly
9. Hateful
10. Dug up
11. Relating to money
12. Not noticeable
13. Without feeling
14. Lean and angler
15. A great fire
16. Sad

| A= | B= | C= | D= |
| E= | F= | G= | H= |
| I= | J= | K= | L= |
| M= | N= | O= | P= |

Dr. Jekyll & Mr. Hyde Vocabulary Magic Squares 1 Answer Key

Match the definition with the vocabulary word. Put your answers in the magic squares below. When your answers are correct, all columns and rows will add to the same number.

A. VOLATILE
B. DETESTABLE
C. INSENSATE
D. UNOBTRUSIVE
E. PECUNIARY
F. GAUNT
G. ENIGMAS
H. REPROVE
I. DISINTERRED
J. CONFLAGRATION
K. INIQUITY
L. AUSTERE
M. SCRUTINY
N. INCIPIENT
O. DISCONSOLATE
P. ODIOUS

1. Hateful; nasty
2. Puzzles
3. Wickedness; injustice
4. Beginning; in an early stage
5. Close examination
6. Strict; stern
7. Rebuke; scold
8. Evaporating rapidly
9. Hateful
10. Dug up
11. Relating to money
12. Not noticeable
13. Without feeling
14. Lean and angler
15. A great fire
16. Sad

| A=8 | B=1 | C=13 | D=12 |
| --- | --- | --- | --- |
| E=11 | F=14 | G=2 | H=7 |
| I=10 | J=15 | K=3 | L=6 |
| M=5 | N=4 | O=16 | P=9 |

Dr. Jekyll & Mr. Hyde Vocabulary Magic Squares 2

Match the definition with the vocabulary word. Put your answers in the magic squares below. When your answers are correct, all columns and rows will add to the same number.

A. SEDULOUSLY
B. CONDONED
C. REPOSE
D. GAUNT
E. PERPLEXITY
F. UNOBTRUSIVE
G. INIQUITY
H. INSENSATE
I. ENIGMAS
J. CAPACIOUS
K. ABJECT
L. CONFLAGRATION
M. SOMBRE
N. EXORBITANT
O. AVERSIONS
P. EFFICACY

1. Without feeling
2. Gloom; depressing
3. Overlooked; forgiven
4. Wretched; lacking pride
5. Large
6. To place trust in
7. Power to produce the desired effect
8. Confusion; puzzlement
9. Firm dislike
10. Not noticeable
11. Puzzles
12. Lean and angler
13. Diligently
14. A great fire
15. Wickedness; injustice
16. Excessive

| A= | B= | C= | D= |
| E= | F= | G= | H= |
| I= | J= | K= | L= |
| M= | N= | O= | P= |

Dr. Jekyll & Mr. Hyde Vocabulary Magic Squares 2 Answer Key

Match the definition with the vocabulary word. Put your answers in the magic squares below. When your answers are correct, all columns and rows will add to the same number.

A. SEDULOUSLY
B. CONDONED
C. REPOSE
D. GAUNT
E. PERPLEXITY
F. UNOBTRUSIVE
G. INIQUITY
H. INSENSATE
I. ENIGMAS
J. CAPACIOUS
K. ABJECT
L. CONFLAGRATION
M. SOMBRE
N. EXORBITANT
O. AVERSIONS
P. EFFICACY

1. Without feeling
2. Gloom; depressing
3. Overlooked; forgiven
4. Wretched; lacking pride
5. Large
6. To place trust in
7. Power to produce the desired effect
8. Confusion; puzzlement
9. Firm dislike
10. Not noticeable
11. Puzzles
12. Lean and angler
13. Diligently
14. A great fire
15. Wickedness; injustice
16. Excessive

| A=13 | B=3 | C=6 | D=12 |
| --- | --- | --- | --- |
| E=8 | F=10 | G=15 | H=1 |
| I=11 | J=5 | K=4 | L=14 |
| M=2 | N=16 | O=9 | P=7 |

Dr. Jekyll & Mr. Hyde Vocabulary Magic Squares 3

Match the definition with the vocabulary word. Put your answers in the magic squares below. When your answers are correct, all columns and rows will add to the same number.

A. GAUNT
B. PECUNIARY
C. MIEN
D. INCOHERENCY
E. CONFLAGRATION
F. EFFICACY
G. INSENSATE
H. INVETERATELY
I. ABJECT
J. MULTIFARIOUS
K. AVERSIONS
L. SCRUTINY
M. CONDONED
N. EMINENTLY
O. AUSTERE
P. ODIOUS

1. Outstanding
2. Without feeling
3. Close examination
4. Lean and angler
5. Firm dislike
6. Relating to money
7. Overlooked; forgiven
8. Deep rooted; habitually
9. A great fire
10. Hateful
11. Behavior; bearing
12. Varied: greatly diversified
13. Unable to express one's thoughts clearly
14. Wretched; lacking pride
15. Power to produce the desired effect
16. Strict; stern

| A= | B= | C= | D= |
|---|---|---|---|
| E= | F= | G= | H= |
| I= | J= | K= | L= |
| M= | N= | O= | P= |

Dr. Jekyll & Mr. Hyde Vocabulary Magic Squares 3 Answer Key

Match the definition with the vocabulary word. Put your answers in the magic squares below. When your answers are correct, all columns and rows will add to the same number.

A. GAUNT
B. PECUNIARY
C. MIEN
D. INCOHERENCY
E. CONFLAGRATION
F. EFFICACY
G. INSENSATE
H. INVETERATELY
I. ABJECT
J. MULTIFARIOUS
K. AVERSIONS
L. SCRUTINY
M. CONDONED
N. EMINENTLY
O. AUSTERE
P. ODIOUS

1. Outstanding
2. Without feeling
3. Close examination
4. Lean and angler
5. Firm dislike
6. Relating to money
7. Overlooked; forgiven
8. Deep rooted; habitually
9. A great fire
10. Hateful
11. Behavior; bearing
12. Varied: greatly diversified
13. Unable to express one's thoughts clearly
14. Wretched; lacking pride
15. Power to produce the desired effect
16. Strict; stern

| A=4 | B=6 | C=11 | D=13 |
| --- | --- | --- | --- |
| E=9 | F=15 | G=2 | H=8 |
| I=14 | J=12 | K=5 | L=3 |
| M=7 | N=1 | O=16 | P=10 |

Dr. Jekyll & Mr. Hyde Vocabulary Magic Squares 4

Match the definition with the vocabulary word. Put your answers in the magic squares below. When your answers are correct, all columns and rows will add to the same number.

A. EFFICACY
B. PERENNIAL
C. SCRUTINY
D. PROTEGE
E. REPROVE
F. EMINENTLY
G. PERPLEXITY
H. MIEN
I. CALAMITY
J. PECUNIARY
K. GAUNT
L. INCOHERENCY
M. CAPACIOUS
N. IMPERIOUS
O. REPOSE
P. LAMENTATION

1. Large
2. Outstanding
3. Behavior; bearing
4. To place trust in
5. Unable to express one's thoughts clearly
6. Close examination
7. Power to produce the desired effect
8. Relating to money
9. Lean and angler
10. A person under the support of a patron
11. Continuing: recurring
12. Disaster
13. Domineering; arrogant
14. Rebuke; scold
15. Confusion; puzzlement
16. Grieving; expressing sorrow

| A= | B= | C= | D= |
| E= | F= | G= | H= |
| I= | J= | K= | L= |
| M= | N= | O= | P= |

Dr. Jekyll & Mr. Hyde Vocabulary Magic Squares 4 Answer Key

Match the definition with the vocabulary word. Put your answers in the magic squares below. When your answers are correct, all columns and rows will add to the same number.

A. EFFICACY
B. PERENNIAL
C. SCRUTINY
D. PROTEGE
E. REPROVE
F. EMINENTLY

G. PERPLEXITY
H. MIEN
I. CALAMITY
J. PECUNIARY
K. GAUNT
L. INCOHERENCY

M. CAPACIOUS
N. IMPERIOUS
O. REPOSE
P. LAMENTATION

1. Large
2. Outstanding
3. Behavior; bearing
4. To place trust in
5. Unable to express one's thoughts clearly
6. Close examination
7. Power to produce the desired effect
8. Relating to money
9. Lean and angler
10. A person under the support of a patron
11. Continuing: recurring
12. Disaster
13. Domineering; arrogant
14. Rebuke; scold
15. Confusion; puzzlement
16. Grieving; expressing sorrow

| A=7 | B=11 | C=6 | D=10 |
|---|---|---|---|
| E=14 | F=2 | G=15 | H=3 |
| I=12 | J=8 | K=9 | L=5 |
| M=1 | N=13 | O=4 | P=16 |

# Dr. Jekyll & Mr. Hyde Vocabulary Word Search 1

```
D I N I Q U I T Y T I X E L P R E P P F
E I P E R E N N I A L M Z F Q G N Q K D
X D S V O L A T I L E D P N F V W B R K
O E C I U D S B N P H C T E F I H Y C V
R T A Y N E A C C O S T E D R D C M D H
B E L Y O T S T O F C H C L T I S A Q P
I S A K B A E Y H P J G Y A B S O H C R
T T M C T N B R E Q K H H M R C Z U B Y
A A I I R I Q X R H L H T E P O M F S W
N B T N U M N K E E L Z P N F N M G G L
T L Y C S U E R N K D S C T P S M K S R
L E B I I R N V C I U V K A G O X Y O W
E D S P V L I M Y O N Q Q T G L R B M X
K M V I E Y G Y I F O C V I Q A J Q B B
C D I E T C M R R V D O O I T U F R J
N A L N D W A S C R U T I N Y E F N E G
P B P T E F S B R M R D U O G X D T T C
F R G A I N E C D N I C B Y U R A H Z J
A L O T C V T E X E E B B E S U J H B
Q B L T O I N L S P R M N P N C T O Y Q
R U J R E O O Y E K C S E D Q Q R U V
M Q P E D G P U T Y Y L S U O L U D E S
J E C N C E E S S G G N B R W P Q R M W
R S O P R T U J T L I X X B E G Z V C L
J C L K P A V E R S I O N S D Z D K M Z
```

A person under the support of a patron (7)
Absurd; incompatible (11)
Beginning; in an early stage (9)
Behavior; bearing (4)
Close examination (8)
Confusion; puzzlement (10)
Continuing: recurring (9)
Diligently (10)
Disaster (8)
Domineering; arrogant (9)
Dug up (11)
Evaporating rapidly (8)
Excessive (10)
Firm dislike (9)
Gloom; depressing (6)
Grieving; expressing sorrow (11)
Hateful (6)
Hateful; nasty (10)
Large (9)
Lean and angler (5)
Not noticeable (11)
Outstanding (9)
Overlooked; forgiven (8)

Pondered; reflected over and over (9)
Power to produce the desired effect (8)
Provided (7)
Puzzles (7)
Rebuke; scold (7)
Relating to money (9)
Sad (12)
Spoke to first (8)
Strict; stern (7)
To place trust in (6)
Unable to express one's thoughts clearly (11)
Varied: greatly diversified (12)
Wickedness; injustice (8)
Without feeling (9)
Wretched; lacking pride (6)

## Dr. Jekyll & Mr. Hyde Vocabulary Word Search 1 Answer Key

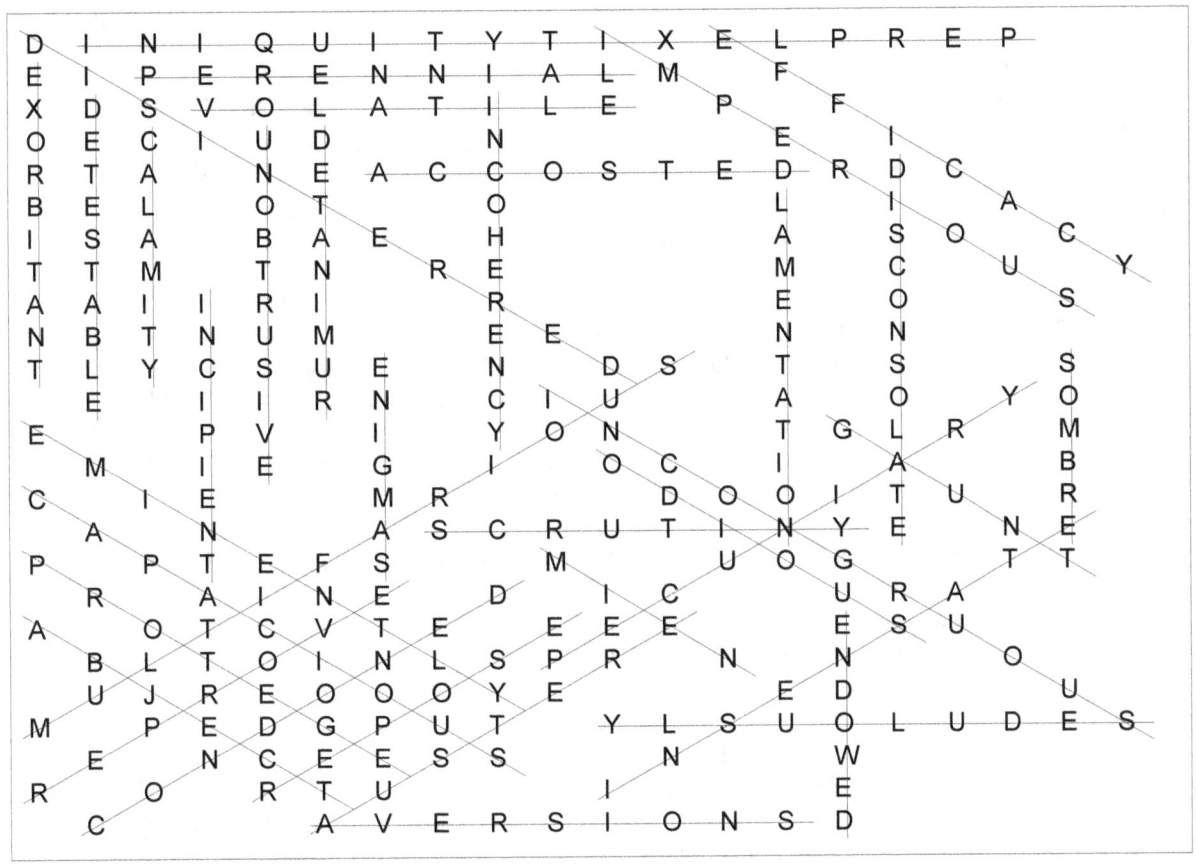

A person under the support of a patron (7)
Absurd; incompatible (11)
Beginning; in an early stage (9)
Behavior; bearing (4)
Close examination (8)
Confusion; puzzlement (10)
Continuing: recurring (9)
Diligently (10)
Disaster (8)
Domineering; arrogant (9)
Dug up (11)
Evaporating rapidly (8)
Excessive (10)
Firm dislike (9)
Gloom; depressing (6)
Grieving; expressing sorrow (11)
Hateful (6)
Hateful; nasty (10)
Large (9)
Lean and angler (5)
Not noticeable (11)
Outstanding (9)
Overlooked; forgiven (8)

Pondered; reflected over and over (9)
Power to produce the desired effect (8)
Provided (7)
Puzzles (7)
Rebuke; scold (7)
Relating to money (9)
Sad (12)
Spoke to first (8)
Strict; stern (7)
To place trust in (6)
Unable to express one's thoughts clearly (11)
Varied: greatly diversified (12)
Wickedness; injustice (8)
Without feeling (9)
Wretched; lacking pride (6)

# Dr. Jekyll & Mr. Hyde Vocabulary Word Search 2

```
U N O B T R U S I V E I N C I P I E N T
J Q B N X V Y Y O M N N O L P B D J K Q
M P X V Q T M L Y G I V I Z E G N D B C
D E T E S T A B L E G E T D C H V J N P
N R K S N T B D F B M T A I U I X V H C
K P M F I S M H C Y A E R S N N S K Y B
J L K L L P R F G S S R G C I C E G A W
H E E E L K U S V K C A A O A O D L V T
F X G F P N M P T S T L N R H U D E K
C I B F C K I D R U N E F S Y E L E R Q
F T Q I R C N Q G O A L N O H R O W S B
V Y N C G S A V V I T Y O L B E U O I Z
A S W A O K T K J C I E C A R N S D O Z
G C U C R N E J T A B W G T D C L N N Z
X N C Y L R D R E P R O V E S Y Y E S G
T P X O E C S O E A O B R U T N T U U D
C M V T S V L R N C X R O I I A O H O G
A S S K L T E R P E E I U T S U C T I D
L U P D W N E R F T Q U N R Q C M R V
A B H S N P H D N O I R E G H E Y I E K
M T S I O S D I R N C S N X J R X E P C
I N A S D B S F I S N O S B S B S N M F
T L E G K I J D J I C W A R J M L V I R
Y F Z H D D E M I N E N T L Y O M R Q D
X Y Y W M U L T I F A R I O U S P M P F
```

A great fire (13)
A person under the support of a patron (7)
Absurd; incompatible (11)
Beginning; in an early stage (9)
Behavior; bearing (4)
Close examination (8)
Confusion; puzzlement (10)
Continuing: recurring (9)
Deep rooted; habitually (12)
Diligently (10)
Disaster (8)
Domineering; arrogant (9)
Dug up (11)
Evaporating rapidly (8)
Excessive (10)
Firm dislike (9)
Gloom; depressing (6)
Hateful (6)
Hateful; nasty (10)
Large (9)
Lean and angler (5)
Not noticeable (11)
Outstanding (9)

Overlooked; forgiven (8)
Pondered; reflected over and over (9)
Power to produce the desired effect (8)
Provided (7)
Puzzles (7)
Rebuke; scold (7)
Relating to money (9)
Sad (12)
Spoke to first (8)
Strict; stern (7)
To place trust in (6)
Unable to express one's thoughts clearly (11)
Varied: greatly diversified (12)
Wickedness; injustice (8)
Without feeling (9)
Wretched; lacking pride (6)

# Dr. Jekyll & Mr. Hyde Vocabulary Word Search 2 Answer Key

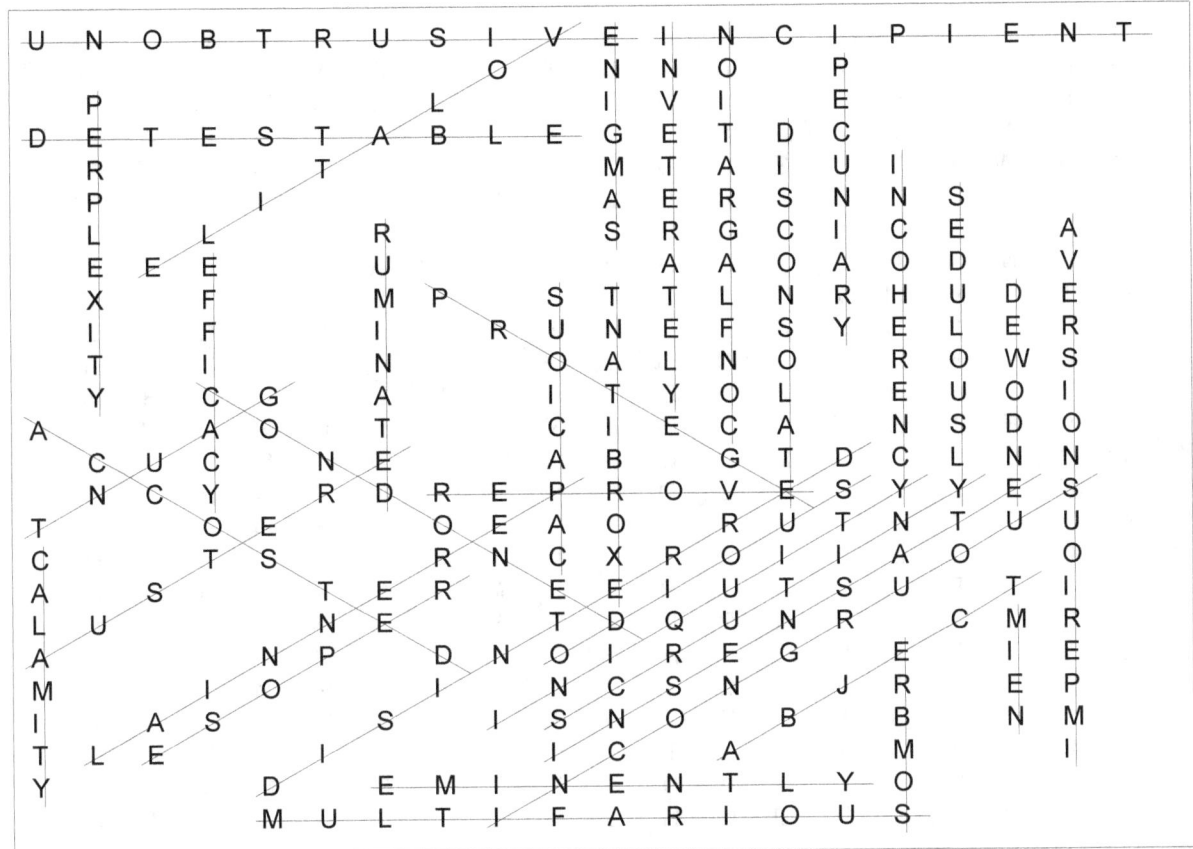

A great fire (13)
A person under the support of a patron (7)
Absurd; incompatible (11)
Beginning; in an early stage (9)
Behavior; bearing (4)
Close examination (8)
Confusion; puzzlement (10)
Continuing: recurring (9)
Deep rooted; habitually (12)
Diligently (10)
Disaster (8)
Domineering; arrogant (9)
Dug up (11)
Evaporating rapidly (8)
Excessive (10)
Firm dislike (9)
Gloom; depressing (6)
Hateful (6)
Hateful; nasty (10)
Large (9)
Lean and angler (5)
Not noticeable (11)
Outstanding (9)

Overlooked; forgiven (8)
Pondered; reflected over and over (9)
Power to produce the desired effect (8)
Provided (7)
Puzzles (7)
Rebuke; scold (7)
Relating to money (9)
Sad (12)
Spoke to first (8)
Strict; stern (7)
To place trust in (6)
Unable to express one's thoughts clearly (11)
Varied: greatly diversified (12)
Wickedness; injustice (8)
Without feeling (9)
Wretched; lacking pride (6)

# Dr. Jekyll & Mr. Hyde Vocabulary Word Search 3

| ABJECT | EFFICACY | INIQUITY | PROTEGE |
|---|---|---|---|
| ACCOSTED | EMINENTLY | INSENSATE | REPOSE |
| AUSTERE | ENDOWED | INVETERATELY | REPROVE |
| AVERSIONS | ENIGMAS | LAMENTATION | RUMINATED |
| CALAMITY | EXORBITANT | MIEN | SCRUTINY |
| CAPACIOUS | GAUNT | MULTIFARIOUS | SEDULOUSLY |
| CONDONED | IMPERIOUS | ODIOUS | SOMBRE |
| DETESTABLE | INCIPIENT | PECUNIARY | VOLATILE |
| DISCONSOLATE | INCOHERENCY | PERENNIAL | |
| DISINTERRED | INCONGRUOUS | PERPLEXITY | |

# Dr. Jekyll & Mr. Hyde Vocabulary Word Search 3

```
V D I S C O N S O L A T E D    L           C
 P O E     A        I   E      A           A
  E L B    P      N W   N                D L
  R A A   T    A S O N  C              E R A
  P M T      E C N N Y              Y   R M
  L E S      I N I E Y          P       R I
  E N E     S L R O C         R   Y   E T T
  X T T  T  A   E E A U        A     E N Y
  I A   A   M   P   C S I       S    E I
  T T  G  G   I   N E         R      S
  Y I    N F   C U          E
    O    I E     Y L T N E N I   M
  I N V E T E R A T E L Y S     O S D   E
  T      E X P O R U E        I   U     S
   N    H O S R A V M S    E O   O   D
    C   O E   B O I R G     N     E
   N  O R Y I Y R I E M R D N
   I P B N T N P V T T P A O
     E M C G I E I A O A F E D T
   R O   E T R   Q R   I N N R M E
    S   J   U    U P T   O T   I   D
       B R        O   L C          O E
  A C C O S T E D  U  I T          U   N
     S          M    S T           S   S
                        Y
```

ABJECT            EFFICACY          INIQUITY          PROTEGE
ACCOSTED          EMINENTLY         INSENSATE         REPOSE
AUSTERE           ENDOWED           INVETERATELY      REPROVE
AVERSIONS         ENIGMAS           LAMENTATION       RUMINATED
CALAMITY          EXORBITANT        MIEN              SCRUTINY
CAPACIOUS         GAUNT             MULTIFARIOUS      SEDULOUSLY
CONDONED          IMPERIOUS         ODIOUS            SOMBRE
DETESTABLE        INCIPIENT         PECUNIARY         VOLATILE
DISCONSOLATE      INCOHERENCY       PERENNIAL
DISINTERRED       INCONGRUOUS       PERPLEXITY

# Dr. Jekyll & Mr. Hyde Vocabulary Word Search 4

```
U N O B T R U S I V E F F I C A C Y N Z
E C M Y L E T A R E T E V N I V B L K H
X O U T N R J M I N C O H E R E N C Y R
O N L L C X F G B W Q V S R P R D H S Q
R F T P Y N X I G D B Q T W T S I T C Z
B L I S E L S N W Q P K Y L K I S P D K
I A F M V R D E T A N I M U R O I V K V
T G A W F R P Q R J S G W S S N N T S H
A R R T A N L V D D L C R O S T A C C
N A I N C I P I E N T R G Y D V E B O J
T T O J C S P T B X U Z G L I R R J N V
N I U B O W E R Y T I J H A O C R E S M
I O S X S S I L I V W T Y M U R E C O L
L N O I T A T N E M A L Y R S N D T L P
S B S A E Q Y E I Z Y T G O Y E T D A R
G E B E D R A I V Q I V M N N C P R T L
E L D Y N U E M M M U B P O R A P Y E G
E N Z U S S J P A P R I D V V P R L R P
W R D T L W A L O E E N T O Z A F T S P
D K E O S O A T G S O R L Y I C X N M K
Y R S P W C U E E C E A I N C I Q E S V
E L Q S R E T S G S T V U O G O M N G G
Z D R J N O D C L I V C L X U U S I W T
L X Q R R J V S L Y E T Z Q Z S K M L F
V J T P B H L E V P L A I N N E R E P Q
```

ABJECT  
ACCOSTED  
AUSTERE  
AVERSIONS  
CALAMITY  
CAPACIOUS  
CONDONED  
CONFLAGRATION  
DETESTABLE  
DISCONSOLATE  

DISINTERRED  
EFFICACY  
EMINENTLY  
ENDOWED  
ENIGMAS  
EXORBITANT  
GAUNT  
IMPERIOUS  
INCIPIENT  
INCOHERENCY  

INIQUITY  
INSENSATE  
INVETERATELY  
LAMENTATION  
MIEN  
MULTIFARIOUS  
ODIOUS  
PECUNIARY  
PERENNIAL  
PERPLEXITY  

PROTEGE  
REPOSE  
REPROVE  
RUMINATED  
SCRUTINY  
SEDULOUSLY  
SOMBRE  
UNOBTRUSIVE  
VOLATILE

# Dr. Jekyll & Mr. Hyde Vocabulary Word Search 4 Answer Key

| ABJECT | DISINTERRED | INIQUITY | PROTEGE |
| ACCOSTED | EFFICACY | INSENSATE | REPOSE |
| AUSTERE | EMINENTLY | INVETERATELY | REPROVE |
| AVERSIONS | ENDOWED | LAMENTATION | RUMINATED |
| CALAMITY | ENIGMAS | MIEN | SCRUTINY |
| CAPACIOUS | EXORBITANT | MULTIFARIOUS | SEDULOUSLY |
| CONDONED | GAUNT | ODIOUS | SOMBRE |
| CONFLAGRATION | IMPERIOUS | PECUNIARY | UNOBTRUSIVE |
| DETESTABLE | INCIPIENT | PERENNIAL | VOLATILE |
| DISCONSOLATE | INCOHERENCY | PERPLEXITY | |

# Dr. Jekyll & Mr. Hyde Vocabulary Crossword 1

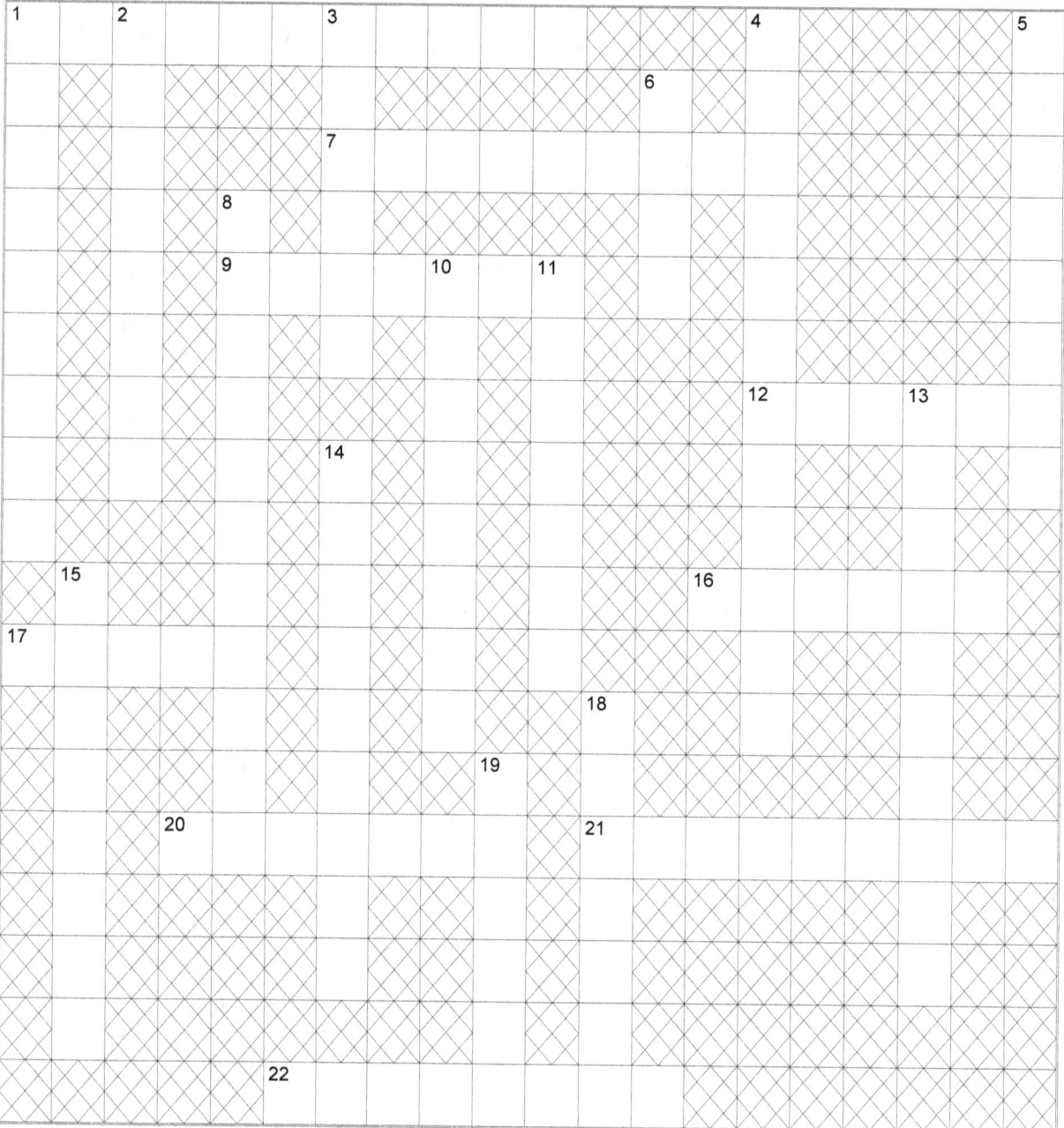

**Across**
1. Unable to express one's thoughts clearly
7. Continuing: recurring
9. Strict; stern
12. Wretched; lacking pride
16. Gloom; depressing
17. Lean and angler
20. Provided
21. Relating to money
22. Spoke to first

**Down**
1. Beginning; in an early stage
2. Overlooked; forgiven
3. To place trust in
4. Varied: greatly diversified
5. Wickedness; injustice
6. Behavior; bearing
8. Grieving; expressing sorrow
10. Power to produce the desired effect
11. Puzzles
13. Excessive
14. Domineering; arrogant
15. Disaster
18. Rebuke; scold
19. Hateful

# Dr. Jekyll & Mr. Hyde Vocabulary Crossword 1 Answer Key

|   | 1 I | N | 2 C | O | 3 H | E | R | E | N | C | Y |   | 4 M |   |   | 5 I |
|---|---|---|---|---|---|---|---|---|---|---|---|---|---|---|---|---|
|   | N |   | O |   | E |   |   |   |   | 6 M |   | U |   |   | N |
|   | C |   | N |   | 7 P | E | R | E | N | N | I | A | L |   |   | I |
|   | I |   | D |   | 8 L | O |   |   |   |   | E |   | T |   |   | Q |
|   | P |   | O |   | 9 A | U | S | T | 10 E | R | 11 E |   | N |   |   | I |   | U |
|   | I |   | N |   | M |   | E |   | F |   | N |   | F |   |   | I |
|   | E |   | E |   | E |   |   | F |   | I |   |   | 12 A | B | J | 13 E | C | T |
|   | N |   | D |   | N |   | 14 I |   | I |   | G |   | R |   | X |   | Y |
|   | T |   |   |   | T |   | M |   | C |   | M |   | I |   | O |   |
|   |   | 15 C |   | A |   | P |   | A |   | A |   | 16 S | O | M | B | R | E |
|   | 17 G | A | U | N | T |   | E |   | C |   | S |   | U |   | B |   |
|   |   | L |   |   | I |   | R |   | Y |   | 18 R |   | S |   | I |   |
|   |   | A |   |   | O |   | I |   |   | 19 O | E |   |   |   | T |   |
|   |   | M |   | 20 E | N | D | O | W | E | D |   | 21 P | E | C | U | N | I | A | R | Y |
|   |   | I |   |   | U |   |   |   | I |   | R |   |   |   | N |   |
|   |   | T |   |   | S |   |   |   | O |   | O |   |   |   | T |   |
|   |   | Y |   |   |   |   |   |   | U |   | V |   |   |   |   |   |
|   |   |   |   | 22 A | C | C | O | S | T | E | D |   |   |   |   |   |

Across
1. Unable to express one's thoughts clearly
7. Continuing: recurring
9. Strict; stern
12. Wretched; lacking pride
16. Gloom; depressing
17. Lean and angler
20. Provided
21. Relating to money
22. Spoke to first

Down
1. Beginning; in an early stage
2. Overlooked; forgiven
3. To place trust in
4. Varied: greatly diversified
5. Wickedness; injustice
6. Behavior; bearing
8. Grieving; expressing sorrow
10. Power to produce the desired effect
11. Puzzles
13. Excessive
14. Domineering; arrogant
15. Disaster
18. Rebuke; scold
19. Hateful

# Dr. Jekyll & Mr. Hyde Vocabulary Crossword 2

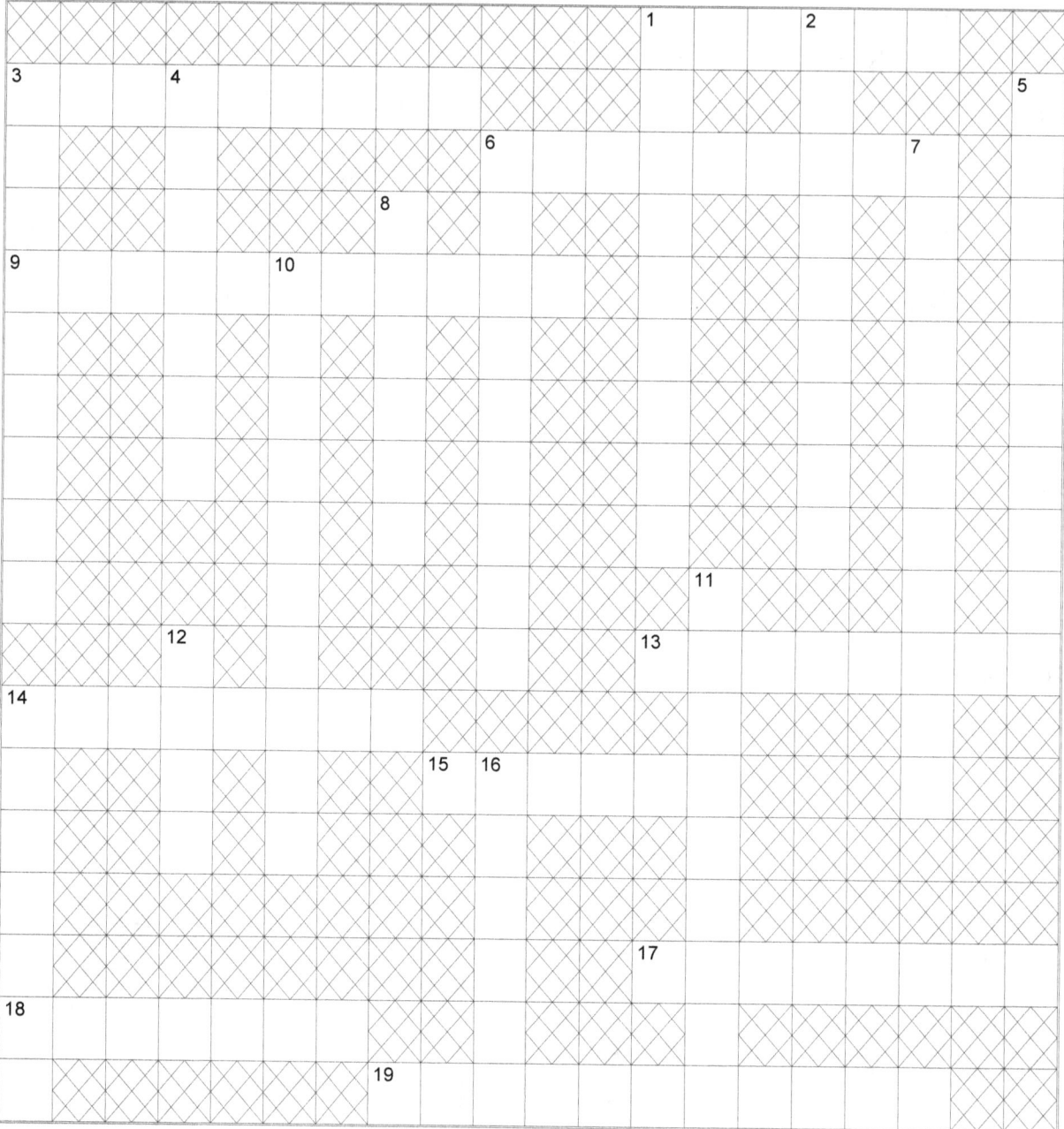

**Across**
1. Wretched; lacking pride
3. Domineering; arrogant
6. Continuing; recurring
9. Unable to express one's thoughts clearly
13. Wickedness; injustice
14. Power to produce the desired effect
15. Gloom; depressing
17. Disaster
18. Strict; stern
19. Dug up

**Down**
1. Firm dislike
2. Outstanding
3. Beginning; in an early stage
4. Provided
5. Diligently
6. Relating to money
7. Grieving; expressing sorrow
8. To place trust in
10. Excessive
11. Without feeling
12. Behavior; bearing
14. Puzzles
16. Hateful

# Dr. Jekyll & Mr. Hyde Vocabulary Crossword 2 Answer Key

**Across**
1. Wretched; lacking pride
3. Domineering; arrogant
6. Continuing; recurring
9. Unable to express one's thoughts clearly
13. Wickedness; injustice
14. Power to produce the desired effect
15. Gloom; depressing
17. Disaster
18. Strict; stern
19. Dug up

**Down**
1. Firm dislike
2. Outstanding
3. Beginning; in an early stage
4. Provided
5. Diligently
6. Relating to money
7. Grieving; expressing sorrow
8. To place trust in
10. Excessive
11. Without feeling
12. Behavior; bearing
14. Puzzles
16. Hateful

# Dr. Jekyll & Mr. Hyde Vocabulary Crossword 3

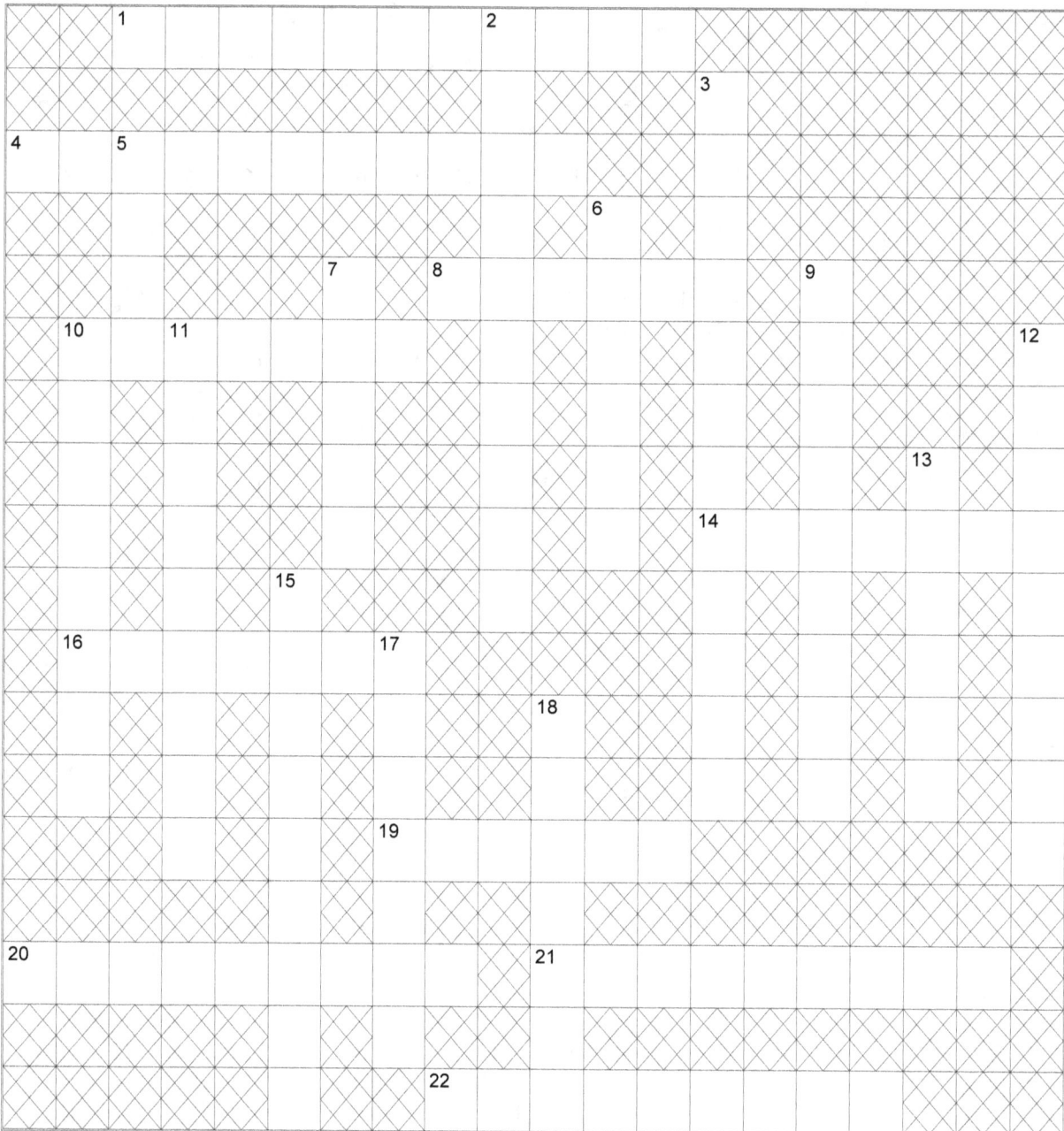

**Across**
1. Unable to express one's thoughts clearly
4. Grieving; expressing sorrow
8. Wretched; lacking pride
10. Puzzles
14. Rebuke; scold
16. Strict; stern
19. Hateful
20. Pondered; reflected over and over
21. Outstanding
22. Firm dislike

**Down**
2. Excessive
3. Varied: greatly diversified
5. Behavior; bearing
6. To place trust in
7. Lean and angler
9. Beginning; in an early stage
10. Power to produce the desired effect
11. Without feeling
12. Continuing: recurring
13. Gloom; depressing
15. Relating to money
17. Provided
18. A person under the support of a patron

# Dr. Jekyll & Mr. Hyde Vocabulary Crossword 3 Answer Key

**Across**
1. Unable to express one's thoughts clearly
4. Grieving; expressing sorrow
8. Wretched; lacking pride
10. Puzzles
14. Rebuke; scold
16. Strict; stern
19. Hateful
20. Pondered; reflected over and over
21. Outstanding
22. Firm dislike

**Down**
2. Excessive
3. Varied: greatly diversified
5. Behavior; bearing
6. To place trust in
7. Lean and angler
9. Beginning; in an early stage
10. Power to produce the desired effect
11. Without feeling
12. Continuing: recurring
13. Gloom; depressing
15. Relating to money
17. Provided
18. A person under the support of a patron

# Dr. Jekyll & Mr. Hyde Vocabulary Crossword 4

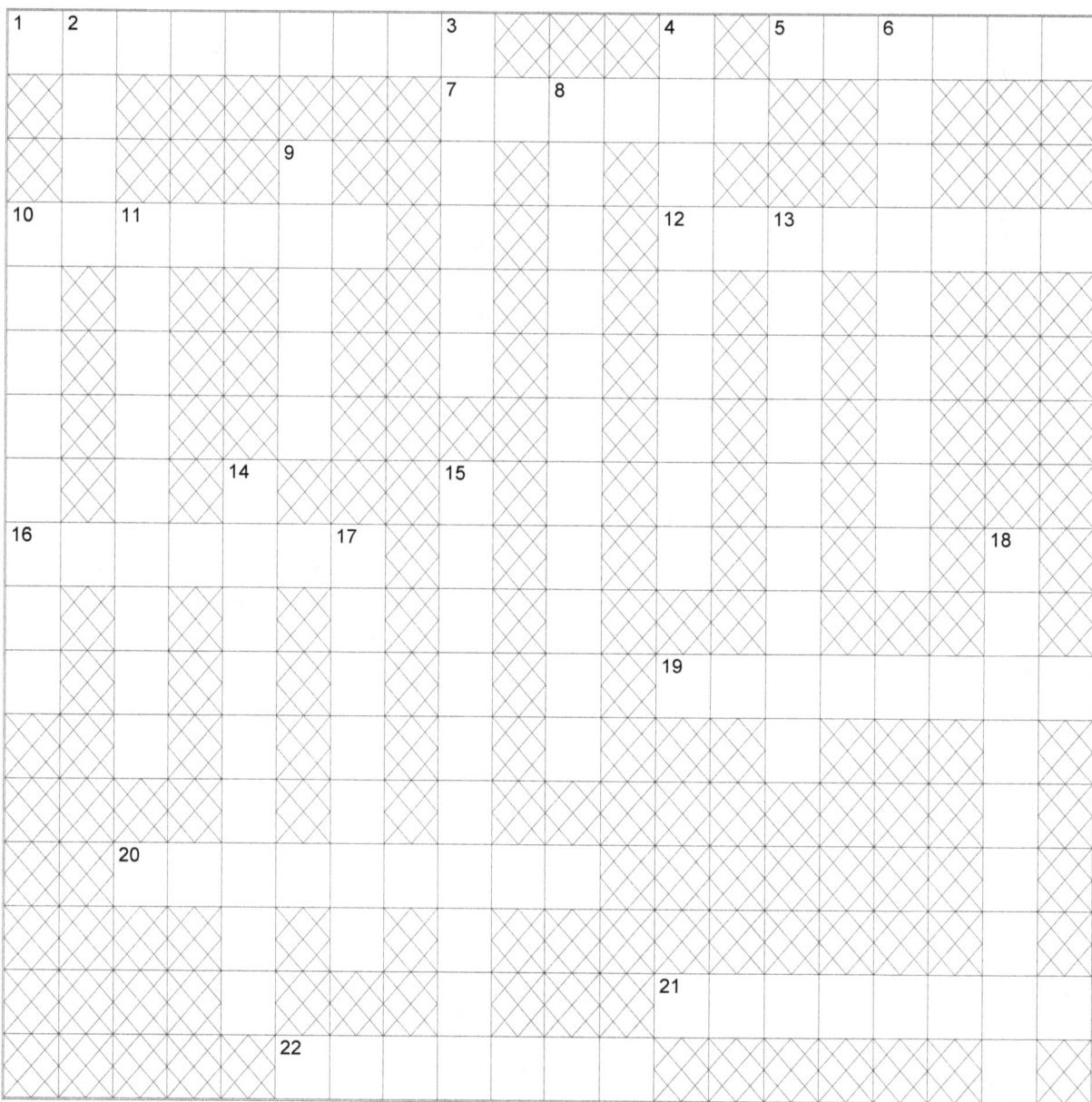

**Across**
1. Domineering; arrogant
5. To place trust in
7. Hateful
10. Puzzles
12. Wickedness; injustice
16. Strict; stern
19. Overlooked; forgiven
20. Outstanding
21. Close examination
22. A person under the support of a patron

**Down**
2. Behavior; bearing
3. Gloom; depressing
4. Pondered; reflected over and over
6. Relating to money
8. Unable to express one's thoughts clearly
9. Lean and angler
10. Power to produce the desired effect
11. Without feeling
13. Beginning; in an early stage
14. Continuing: recurring
15. Excessive
17. Provided
18. Firm dislike

# Dr. Jekyll & Mr. Hyde Vocabulary Crossword 4 Answer Key

|   | 1 I | 2 M | P | E | R | I | O | U | 3 S |   | 4 R |   | 5 R | E | 6 P | O | S | E |
|---|---|---|---|---|---|---|---|---|---|---|---|---|---|---|---|---|---|---|
|   |   | I |   |   |   |   |   | 7 O | 8 D | I | O | U | S |   | E |   |   |   |
|   |   | E |   |   | 9 G |   |   | M |   | N |   | M |   |   | C |   |   |   |
| 10 E | 11 N | I | G | M | A | S |   | B |   | C |   | 12 I | N | 13 I | Q | U | I | T | Y |
|   | F |   | N |   | U |   |   | R |   | O |   | N |   | N |   | N |   |   |
|   | F |   | S |   | N |   |   | E |   | H |   | A |   | C |   | I |   |   |
|   | I |   | E |   | T |   |   |   |   | E |   | T |   | I |   | A |   |   |
|   | C |   | N |   | 14 P |   |   | 15 E |   | R |   | E |   | P |   | R |   | 18 A |
| 16 A | U | S | T | E | R | 17 E |   | X |   | E |   | D |   | I |   | Y |   | V |
| C |   |   | A |   | R | N |   | O |   | N |   |   |   | E |   |   |   | V |
| Y |   |   | T |   | E | D |   | R |   | C |   | 19 C | O | N | D | O | N | E | D |
|   |   |   | E |   | N | O |   | B |   | Y |   | T |   |   |   |   |   | R |
|   |   |   |   |   | N | W |   | I |   |   |   |   |   |   |   |   |   | S |
|   |   |   | 20 E | M | I | N | E | N | T | L | Y |   |   |   |   |   |   | I |
|   |   |   |   |   | A |   | D |   | A |   |   |   |   |   |   |   |   | O |
|   |   |   |   |   | L |   |   |   | N |   |   | 21 S | C | R | U | T | I | N | Y |
|   |   |   | 22 P | R | O | T | E | G | E |   |   |   |   |   |   |   |   | S |

Across
1. Domineering; arrogant
5. To place trust in
7. Hateful
10. Puzzles
12. Wickedness; injustice
16. Strict; stern
19. Overlooked; forgiven
20. Outstanding
21. Close examination
22. A person under the support of a patron

Down
2. Behavior; bearing
3. Gloom; depressing
4. Pondered; reflected over and over
6. Relating to money
8. Unable to express one's thoughts clearly
9. Lean and angler
10. Power to produce the desired effect
11. Without feeling
13. Beginning; in an early stage
14. Continuing: recurring
15. Excessive
17. Provided
18. Firm dislike

Dr. Jekyll & Mr. Hyde Vocabulary Juggle Letters 1

1. ATENNTLAMIO = 1. _____
   Grieving; expressing sorrow

2. ASENESINT = 2. _____
   Without feeling

3. RUVIBSTUOEN = 3. _____
   Not noticeable

4. NOCENDOD = 4. _____
   Overlooked; forgiven

5. EUTESAR = 5. _____
   Strict; stern

6. ETTAELESBD = 6. _____
   Hateful; nasty

7. GRPEETO = 7. _____
   A person under the support of a patron

8. EYAVELRETTIN = 8. _____
   Deep rooted; habitually

9. MPEISURIO = 9. _____
   Domineering; arrogant

10. SDOOIU = 10. _____
    Hateful

11. BATCJE = 11. _____
    Wretched; lacking pride

12. IUATLSIFROUM = 12. _____
    Varied; greatly diversified

13. NIUPYACRE = 13. _____
    Relating to money

14. ICNTNEPII = 14. _____
    Beginning; in an early stage

15. NEDDWOE = 15. _____
    Provided

Dr. Jekyll & Mr. Hyde Vocabulary Juggle Letters 1 Answer Key

1. ATENNTLAMIO = 1. LAMENTATION
   Grieving; expressing sorrow

2. ASENESINT = 2. INSENSATE
   Without feeling

3. RUVIBSTUOEN = 3. UNOBTRUSIVE
   Not noticeable

4. NOCENDOD = 4. CONDONED
   Overlooked; forgiven

5. EUTESAR = 5. AUSTERE
   Strict; stern

6. ETTAELESBD = 6. DETESTABLE
   Hateful; nasty

7. GRPEETO = 7. PROTEGE
   A person under the support of a patron

8. EYAVELRETTIN = 8. INVETERATELY
   Deep rooted; habitually

9. MPEISURIO = 9. IMPERIOUS
   Domineering; arrogant

10. SDOOIU =10. ODIOUS
    Hateful

11. BATCJE =11. ABJECT
    Wretched; lacking pride

12. IUATLSIFROUM =12. MULTIFARIOUS
    Varied: greatly diversified

13. NIUPYACRE =13. PECUNIARY
    Relating to money

14. ICNTNEPII =14. INCIPIENT
    Beginning; in an early stage

15. NEDDWOE =15. ENDOWED
    Provided

Dr. Jekyll & Mr. Hyde Vocabulary Juggle Letters 2

1. ELSOUDYSUL = 1. _____
   Diligently

2. DOCENNOD = 2. _____
   Overlooked; forgiven

3. CPOUAICSA = 3. _____
   Large

4. EIUDATRMN = 4. _____
   Pondered; reflected over and over

5. EROPGET = 5. _____
   A person under the support of a patron

6. CEDASCOT = 6. _____
   Spoke to first

7. ELATEDTEBS = 7. _____
   Hateful; nasty

8. OSMLUIFATUIR = 8. _____
   Varied: greatly diversified

9. IFCYFACE = 9. _____
   Power to produce the desired effect

10. GAIEMNS = 10. _____
    Puzzles

11. IYSCUNRT = 11. _____
    Close examination

12. BJATEC = 12. _____
    Wretched; lacking pride

13. RUESTAE = 13. _____
    Strict; stern

14. ITPLRXYPEE = 14. _____
    Confusion; puzzlement

15. DEWDONE = 15. _____
    Provided

Dr. Jekyll & Mr. Hyde Vocabulary Juggle Letters 2 Answer Key

1. ELSOUDYSUL = 1. SEDULOUSLY
   Diligently

2. DOCENNOD = 2. CONDONED
   Overlooked; forgiven

3. CPOUAICSA = 3. CAPACIOUS
   Large

4. EIUDATRMN = 4. RUMINATED
   Pondered; reflected over and over

5. EROPGET = 5. PROTEGE
   A person under the support of a patron

6. CEDASCOT = 6. ACCOSTED
   Spoke to first

7. ELATEDTEBS = 7. DETESTABLE
   Hateful; nasty

8. OSMLUIFATUIR = 8. MULTIFARIOUS
   Varied: greatly diversified

9. IFCYFACE = 9. EFFICACY
   Power to produce the desired effect

10. GAIEMNS = 10. ENIGMAS
    Puzzles

11. IYSCUNRT = 11. SCRUTINY
    Close examination

12. BJATEC = 12. ABJECT
    Wretched; lacking pride

13. RUESTAE = 13. AUSTERE
    Strict; stern

14. ITPLRXYPEE = 14. PERPLEXITY
    Confusion; puzzlement

15. DEWDONE = 15. ENDOWED
    Provided

Dr. Jekyll & Mr. Hyde Vocabulary Juggle Letters 3

1. UCSYNRTI = 1. _____
   Close examination

2. VPREOER = 2. _____
   Rebuke; scold

3. UNGAT = 3. _____
   Lean and angler

4. TNEOLNAIMTA = 4. _____
   Grieving; expressing sorrow

5. TAYMAILC = 5. _____
   Disaster

6. ETIESNANS = 6. _____
   Without feeling

7. TESEEALDBT = 7. _____
   Hateful; nasty

8. TEYILREANTEV = 8. _____
   Deep rooted; habitually

9. YTEEINLNM = 9. _____
   Outstanding

10. YOULLEDSUS =10. _____
    Diligently

11. OBRTEXTNAI =11. _____
    Excessive

12. DOEDNONC =12. _____
    Overlooked; forgiven

13. COCERYNHINE =13. _____
    Unable to express one's thoughts clearly

14. ANTOILAFOCNRG =14. _____
    A great fire

15. ETVLILOA =15. _____
    Evaporating rapidly

Dr. Jekyll & Mr. Hyde Vocabulary Juggle Letters 3 Answer Key

1. UCSYNRTI = 1. SCRUTINY
   Close examination

2. VPREOER = 2. REPROVE
   Rebuke; scold

3. UNGAT = 3. GAUNT
   Lean and angler

4. TNEOLNAIMTA = 4. LAMENTATION
   Grieving; expressing sorrow

5. TAYMAILC = 5. CALAMITY
   Disaster

6. ETIESNANS = 6. INSENSATE
   Without feeling

7. TESEEALDBT = 7. DETESTABLE
   Hateful; nasty

8. TEYILREANTEV = 8. INVETERATELY
   Deep rooted; habitually

9. YTEEINLNM = 9. EMINENTLY
   Outstanding

10. YOULLEDSUS = 10. SEDULOUSLY
    Diligently

11. OBRTEXTNAI = 11. EXORBITANT
    Excessive

12. DOEDNONC = 12. CONDONED
    Overlooked; forgiven

13. COCERYNHINE = 13. INCOHERENCY
    Unable to express one's thoughts clearly

14. ANTOILAFOCNRG = 14. CONFLAGRATION
    A great fire

15. ETVLILOA = 15. VOLATILE
    Evaporating rapidly

Dr. Jekyll & Mr. Hyde Vocabulary Juggle Letters 4

1. UINNOCSUORG = 1. _____
   Absurd; incompatible

2. EISOMRUIP = 2. _____
   Domineering; arrogant

3. ALTCIMYA = 3. _____
   Disaster

4. TSIUURLOMFIA = 4. _____
   Varied: greatly diversified

5. CCPAUSOIA = 5. _____
   Large

6. ODDNCEON = 6. _____
   Overlooked; forgiven

7. SDIRDRITNEE = 7. _____
   Dug up

8. NRIECYCNHOE = 8. _____
   Unable to express one's thoughts clearly

9. ECTSDAOC = 9. _____
   Spoke to first

10. ERTEUSA = 10. _____
    Strict; stern

11. CNTNEIIPI = 11. _____
    Beginning; in an early stage

12. EOEDNWD = 12. _____
    Provided

13. TALLVIOE = 13. _____
    Evaporating rapidly

14. GTOEPER = 14. _____
    A person under the support of a patron

15. EIPRALNEN = 15. _____
    Continuing: recurring

Dr. Jekyll & Mr. Hyde Vocabulary Juggle Letters 4 Answer Key

1. UINNOCSUORG = 1. INCONGRUOUS
   Absurd; incompatible

2. EISOMRUIP = 2. IMPERIOUS
   Domineering; arrogant

3. ALTCIMYA = 3. CALAMITY
   Disaster

4. TSIUURLOMFIA = 4. MULTIFARIOUS
   Varied: greatly diversified

5. CCPAUSOIA = 5. CAPACIOUS
   Large

6. ODDNCEON = 6. CONDONED
   Overlooked; forgiven

7. SDIRDRITNEE = 7. DISINTERRED
   Dug up

8. NRIECYCNHOE = 8. INCOHERENCY
   Unable to express one's thoughts clearly

9. ECTSDAOC = 9. ACCOSTED
   Spoke to first

10. ERTEUSA = 10. AUSTERE
    Strict; stern

11. CNTNEIIPI = 11. INCIPIENT
    Beginning; in an early stage

12. EOEDNWD = 12. ENDOWED
    Provided

13. TALLVIOE = 13. VOLATILE
    Evaporating rapidly

14. GTOEPER = 14. PROTEGE
    A person under the support of a patron

15. EIPRALNEN = 15. PERENNIAL
    Continuing: recurring

| ABJECT | Wretched; lacking pride |
|---|---|
| ACCOSTED | Spoke to first |
| AUSTERE | Strict; stern |
| AVERSIONS | Firm dislike |
| CALAMITY | Disaster |
| CAPACIOUS | Large |

| | |
|---|---|
| CONDONED | Overlooked; forgiven |
| CONFLAGRATION | A great fire |
| DETESTABLE | Hateful; nasty |
| DISCONSOLATE | Sad |
| DISINTERRED | Dug up |
| EFFICACY | Power to produce the desired effect |

| | |
|---|---|
| EMINENTLY | Outstanding |
| ENDOWED | Provided |
| ENIGMAS | Puzzles |
| EXORBITANT | Excessive |
| GAUNT | Lean and angler |
| IMPERIOUS | Domineering; arrogant |

| | |
|---|---|
| INCIPIENT | Beginning; in an early stage |
| INCOHERENCY | Unable to express one's thoughts clearly |
| INCONGRUOUS | Absurd; incompatible |
| INIQUITY | Wickedness; injustice |
| INSENSATE | Without feeling |
| INVETERATELY | Deep rooted; habitually |

| | |
|---|---|
| LAMENTATION | Grieving; expressing sorrow |
| MIEN | Behavior; bearing |
| MULTIFARIOUS | Varied: greatly diversified |
| ODIOUS | Hateful |
| PECUNIARY | Relating to money |
| PERENNIAL | Continuing: recurring |

| | |
|---|---|
| PERPLEXITY | Confusion; puzzlement |
| PROTEGE | A person under the support of a patron |
| REPOSE | To place trust in |
| REPROVE | Rebuke; scold |
| RUMINATED | Pondered; reflected over and over |
| SCRUTINY | Close examination |

| | |
|---|---|
| SEDULOUSLY | Diligently |
| SOMBRE | Gloom; depressing |
| UNOBTRUSIVE | Not noticeable |
| VOLATILE | Evaporating rapidly |

Dr. Jekyll & Mr. Hyde Vocabulary

| VOLATILE | ACCOSTED | IMPERIOUS | DETESTABLE | RUMINATED |
|---|---|---|---|---|
| REPOSE | INIQUITY | EMINENTLY | INCOHERENCY | ODIOUS |
| AVERSIONS | INSENSATE | FREE SPACE | INVETERATELY | CONFLAGRATION |
| MIEN | REPROVE | ABJECT | DISCONSOLATE | CALAMITY |
| PROTEGE | UNOBTRUSIVE | SEDULOUSLY | SOMBRE | EFFICACY |

Dr. Jekyll & Mr. Hyde Vocabulary

| CAPACIOUS | ENDOWED | SCRUTINY | PECUNIARY | INCONGRUOUS |
|---|---|---|---|---|
| AUSTERE | ENIGMAS | CONDONED | INCIPIENT | PERENNIAL |
| DISINTERRED | MULTIFARIOUS | FREE SPACE | PERPLEXITY | LAMENTATION |
| EFFICACY | SOMBRE | SEDULOUSLY | UNOBTRUSIVE | PROTEGE |
| CALAMITY | DISCONSOLATE | ABJECT | REPROVE | MIEN |

Dr. Jekyll & Mr. Hyde Vocabulary

| AVERSIONS | INIQUITY | EFFICACY | PECUNIARY | REPROVE |
|---|---|---|---|---|
| IMPERIOUS | DISINTERRED | AUSTERE | RUMINATED | PERENNIAL |
| LAMENTATION | DISCONSOLATE | FREE SPACE | CALAMITY | EXORBITANT |
| GAUNT | INCIPIENT | UNOBTRUSIVE | INSENSATE | ENDOWED |
| ACCOSTED | INCOHERENCY | CONFLAGRATION | SCRUTINY | PROTEGE |

Dr. Jekyll & Mr. Hyde Vocabulary

| SOMBRE | MIEN | EMINENTLY | CAPACIOUS | PERPLEXITY |
|---|---|---|---|---|
| ABJECT | INCONGRUOUS | REPOSE | ENIGMAS | VOLATILE |
| INVETERATELY | CONDONED | FREE SPACE | SEDULOUSLY | MULTIFARIOUS |
| PROTEGE | SCRUTINY | CONFLAGRATION | INCOHERENCY | ACCOSTED |
| ENDOWED | INSENSATE | UNOBTRUSIVE | INCIPIENT | GAUNT |

Dr. Jekyll & Mr. Hyde Vocabulary

| EXORBITANT | DISINTERRED | DISCONSOLATE | EMINENTLY | SOMBRE |
|---|---|---|---|---|
| AVERSIONS | MIEN | DETESTABLE | GAUNT | MULTIFARIOUS |
| CALAMITY | INCOHERENCY | FREE SPACE | SEDULOUSLY | CAPACIOUS |
| ABJECT | CONDONED | ACCOSTED | CONFLAGRATION | AUSTERE |
| IMPERIOUS | ENDOWED | SCRUTINY | INIQUITY | PERPLEXITY |

Dr. Jekyll & Mr. Hyde Vocabulary

| PROTEGE | INCONGRUOUS | VOLATILE | REPOSE | EFFICACY |
|---|---|---|---|---|
| PECUNIARY | UNOBTRUSIVE | INVETERATELY | PERENNIAL | RUMINATED |
| INSENSATE | REPROVE | FREE SPACE | ODIOUS | ENIGMAS |
| PERPLEXITY | INIQUITY | SCRUTINY | ENDOWED | IMPERIOUS |
| AUSTERE | CONFLAGRATION | ACCOSTED | CONDONED | ABJECT |

Dr. Jekyll & Mr. Hyde Vocabulary

| PROTEGE | EXORBITANT | SCRUTINY | UNOBTRUSIVE | PECUNIARY |
|---|---|---|---|---|
| INSENSATE | SEDULOUSLY | ACCOSTED | CAPACIOUS | PERENNIAL |
| CONDONED | CALAMITY | FREE SPACE | RUMINATED | VOLATILE |
| EFFICACY | INVETERATELY | MIEN | AVERSIONS | ENDOWED |
| ENIGMAS | INCIPIENT | DETESTABLE | REPOSE | AUSTERE |

Dr. Jekyll & Mr. Hyde Vocabulary

| REPROVE | IMPERIOUS | SOMBRE | LAMENTATION | ABJECT |
|---|---|---|---|---|
| MULTIFARIOUS | ODIOUS | INCONGRUOUS | PERPLEXITY | INCOHERENCY |
| DISCONSOLATE | DISINTERRED | FREE SPACE | INIQUITY | CONFLAGRATION |
| AUSTERE | REPOSE | DETESTABLE | INCIPIENT | ENIGMAS |
| ENDOWED | AVERSIONS | MIEN | INVETERATELY | EFFICACY |

Dr. Jekyll & Mr. Hyde Vocabulary

| ENDOWED | INCOHERENCY | LAMENTATION | EMINENTLY | INIQUITY |
|---|---|---|---|---|
| SEDULOUSLY | ENIGMAS | CONFLAGRATION | DETESTABLE | SCRUTINY |
| PERPLEXITY | INSENSATE | FREE SPACE | CONDONED | RUMINATED |
| PECUNIARY | DISCONSOLATE | INCIPIENT | EFFICACY | AUSTERE |
| PROTEGE | GAUNT | INVETERATELY | MULTIFARIOUS | SOMBRE |

Dr. Jekyll & Mr. Hyde Vocabulary

| ODIOUS | CAPACIOUS | REPROVE | PERENNIAL | REPOSE |
|---|---|---|---|---|
| ABJECT | AVERSIONS | ACCOSTED | VOLATILE | DISINTERRED |
| CALAMITY | UNOBTRUSIVE | FREE SPACE | EXORBITANT | INCONGRUOUS |
| SOMBRE | MULTIFARIOUS | INVETERATELY | GAUNT | PROTEGE |
| AUSTERE | EFFICACY | INCIPIENT | DISCONSOLATE | PECUNIARY |

## Dr. Jekyll & Mr. Hyde Vocabulary

| AVERSIONS | IMPERIOUS | GAUNT | EXORBITANT | ABJECT |
|---|---|---|---|---|
| RUMINATED | ACCOSTED | AUSTERE | SEDULOUSLY | INCONGRUOUS |
| REPOSE | CALAMITY | FREE SPACE | INCOHERENCY | MIEN |
| INIQUITY | INSENSATE | EMINENTLY | REPROVE | CONDONED |
| PERENNIAL | INCIPIENT | MULTIFARIOUS | VOLATILE | CONFLAGRATION |

## Dr. Jekyll & Mr. Hyde Vocabulary

| DISINTERRED | INVETERATELY | UNOBTRUSIVE | PERPLEXITY | DISCONSOLATE |
|---|---|---|---|---|
| ENDOWED | SOMBRE | ODIOUS | EFFICACY | LAMENTATION |
| PROTEGE | PECUNIARY | FREE SPACE | CAPACIOUS | SCRUTINY |
| CONFLAGRATION | VOLATILE | MULTIFARIOUS | INCIPIENT | PERENNIAL |
| CONDONED | REPROVE | EMINENTLY | INSENSATE | INIQUITY |

## Dr. Jekyll & Mr. Hyde Vocabulary

| | | | | |
|---|---|---|---|---|
| AVERSIONS | DISCONSOLATE | IMPERIOUS | REPROVE | EFFICACY |
| EMINENTLY | VOLATILE | PECUNIARY | PROTEGE | DETESTABLE |
| CALAMITY | ENDOWED | FREE SPACE | ODIOUS | PERPLEXITY |
| INIQUITY | MULTIFARIOUS | AUSTERE | INCIPIENT | CONDONED |
| EXORBITANT | INVETERATELY | RUMINATED | INSENSATE | UNOBTRUSIVE |

## Dr. Jekyll & Mr. Hyde Vocabulary

| | | | | |
|---|---|---|---|---|
| LAMENTATION | INCONGRUOUS | ENIGMAS | SEDULOUSLY | DISINTERRED |
| CAPACIOUS | INCOHERENCY | SCRUTINY | MIEN | REPOSE |
| SOMBRE | GAUNT | FREE SPACE | CONFLAGRATION | ABJECT |
| UNOBTRUSIVE | INSENSATE | RUMINATED | INVETERATELY | EXORBITANT |
| CONDONED | INCIPIENT | AUSTERE | MULTIFARIOUS | INIQUITY |

Dr. Jekyll & Mr. Hyde Vocabulary

| INIQUITY | INSENSATE | REPOSE | CALAMITY | ABJECT |
|---|---|---|---|---|
| AVERSIONS | DETESTABLE | MIEN | EMINENTLY | DISCONSOLATE |
| MULTIFARIOUS | ENDOWED | FREE SPACE | AUSTERE | INCIPIENT |
| INVETERATELY | EXORBITANT | DISINTERRED | SEDULOUSLY | IMPERIOUS |
| ACCOSTED | ENIGMAS | PROTEGE | CONDONED | ODIOUS |

Dr. Jekyll & Mr. Hyde Vocabulary

| RUMINATED | SCRUTINY | CONFLAGRATION | EFFICACY | PERPLEXITY |
|---|---|---|---|---|
| CAPACIOUS | SOMBRE | INCOHERENCY | REPROVE | PECUNIARY |
| LAMENTATION | UNOBTRUSIVE | FREE SPACE | VOLATILE | PERENNIAL |
| ODIOUS | CONDONED | PROTEGE | ENIGMAS | ACCOSTED |
| IMPERIOUS | SEDULOUSLY | DISINTERRED | EXORBITANT | INVETERATELY |

Dr. Jekyll & Mr. Hyde Vocabulary

| AUSTERE | REPROVE | ABJECT | VOLATILE | IMPERIOUS |
|---|---|---|---|---|
| PECUNIARY | PROTEGE | GAUNT | INVETERATELY | ENIGMAS |
| ENDOWED | DISCONSOLATE | FREE SPACE | SCRUTINY | MULTIFARIOUS |
| REPOSE | INSENSATE | CAPACIOUS | ODIOUS | DISINTERRED |
| INIQUITY | EFFICACY | CONDONED | DETESTABLE | UNOBTRUSIVE |

Dr. Jekyll & Mr. Hyde Vocabulary

| ACCOSTED | RUMINATED | EMINENTLY | INCOHERENCY | LAMENTATION |
|---|---|---|---|---|
| INCIPIENT | PERPLEXITY | INCONGRUOUS | PERENNIAL | CONFLAGRATION |
| SOMBRE | MIEN | FREE SPACE | EXORBITANT | SEDULOUSLY |
| UNOBTRUSIVE | DETESTABLE | CONDONED | EFFICACY | INIQUITY |
| DISINTERRED | ODIOUS | CAPACIOUS | INSENSATE | REPOSE |

## Dr. Jekyll & Mr. Hyde Vocabulary

| SOMBRE | INCIPIENT | DISINTERRED | EFFICACY | INVETERATELY |
|---|---|---|---|---|
| INSENSATE | SCRUTINY | INCONGRUOUS | IMPERIOUS | EXORBITANT |
| PERPLEXITY | DETESTABLE | FREE SPACE | ACCOSTED | SEDULOUSLY |
| PECUNIARY | UNOBTRUSIVE | CALAMITY | MULTIFARIOUS | VOLATILE |
| INCOHERENCY | INIQUITY | RUMINATED | REPROVE | CAPACIOUS |

## Dr. Jekyll & Mr. Hyde Vocabulary

| REPOSE | CONFLAGRATION | ABJECT | ENIGMAS | AUSTERE |
|---|---|---|---|---|
| PERENNIAL | MIEN | LAMENTATION | CONDONED | ODIOUS |
| EMINENTLY | ENDOWED | FREE SPACE | PROTEGE | AVERSIONS |
| CAPACIOUS | REPROVE | RUMINATED | INIQUITY | INCOHERENCY |
| VOLATILE | MULTIFARIOUS | CALAMITY | UNOBTRUSIVE | PECUNIARY |

## Dr. Jekyll & Mr. Hyde Vocabulary

| INCOHERENCY | INCIPIENT | VOLATILE | ENIGMAS | GAUNT |
|---|---|---|---|---|
| PECUNIARY | SOMBRE | CALAMITY | CONFLAGRATION | SEDULOUSLY |
| ODIOUS | EXORBITANT | FREE SPACE | PERPLEXITY | INVETERATELY |
| REPROVE | EFFICACY | AUSTERE | PERENNIAL | PROTEGE |
| MULTIFARIOUS | DISCONSOLATE | CAPACIOUS | LAMENTATION | INIQUITY |

## Dr. Jekyll & Mr. Hyde Vocabulary

| EMINENTLY | ABJECT | CONDONED | AVERSIONS | RUMINATED |
|---|---|---|---|---|
| SCRUTINY | MIEN | INSENSATE | ACCOSTED | INCONGRUOUS |
| REPOSE | DETESTABLE | FREE SPACE | IMPERIOUS | DISINTERRED |
| INIQUITY | LAMENTATION | CAPACIOUS | DISCONSOLATE | MULTIFARIOUS |
| PROTEGE | PERENNIAL | AUSTERE | EFFICACY | REPROVE |

## Dr. Jekyll & Mr. Hyde Vocabulary

| INSENSATE | SEDULOUSLY | INCONGRUOUS | UNOBTRUSIVE | PERENNIAL |
|---|---|---|---|---|
| LAMENTATION | MULTIFARIOUS | CAPACIOUS | REPOSE | CONDONED |
| INVETERATELY | INCIPIENT | FREE SPACE | REPROVE | MIEN |
| ACCOSTED | RUMINATED | PERPLEXITY | ODIOUS | EXORBITANT |
| DETESTABLE | INIQUITY | ENIGMAS | CALAMITY | INCOHERENCY |

## Dr. Jekyll & Mr. Hyde Vocabulary

| AUSTERE | ABJECT | DISCONSOLATE | CONFLAGRATION | IMPERIOUS |
|---|---|---|---|---|
| SOMBRE | SCRUTINY | ENDOWED | AVERSIONS | DISINTERRED |
| VOLATILE | EFFICACY | FREE SPACE | PROTEGE | GAUNT |
| INCOHERENCY | CALAMITY | ENIGMAS | INIQUITY | DETESTABLE |
| EXORBITANT | ODIOUS | PERPLEXITY | RUMINATED | ACCOSTED |

Dr. Jekyll & Mr. Hyde Vocabulary

| VOLATILE | RUMINATED | PERENNIAL | INSENSATE | EFFICACY |
|---|---|---|---|---|
| INIQUITY | LAMENTATION | CONFLAGRATION | AVERSIONS | PROTEGE |
| CAPACIOUS | ODIOUS | FREE SPACE | EXORBITANT | ENIGMAS |
| REPROVE | SEDULOUSLY | CONDONED | IMPERIOUS | GAUNT |
| CALAMITY | SCRUTINY | DETESTABLE | INCONGRUOUS | ENDOWED |

Dr. Jekyll & Mr. Hyde Vocabulary

| UNOBTRUSIVE | INCOHERENCY | SOMBRE | PECUNIARY | REPOSE |
|---|---|---|---|---|
| MIEN | PERPLEXITY | ABJECT | MULTIFARIOUS | DISCONSOLATE |
| AUSTERE | ACCOSTED | FREE SPACE | INVETERATELY | EMINENTLY |
| ENDOWED | INCONGRUOUS | DETESTABLE | SCRUTINY | CALAMITY |
| GAUNT | IMPERIOUS | CONDONED | SEDULOUSLY | REPROVE |

Dr. Jekyll & Mr. Hyde Vocabulary

| INSENSATE | IMPERIOUS | GAUNT | SCRUTINY | RUMINATED |
|---|---|---|---|---|
| DISINTERRED | INCOHERENCY | REPOSE | SEDULOUSLY | EMINENTLY |
| ENIGMAS | UNOBTRUSIVE | FREE SPACE | DETESTABLE | CONDONED |
| REPROVE | CONFLAGRATION | MIEN | CAPACIOUS | PROTEGE |
| ABJECT | PECUNIARY | DISCONSOLATE | EXORBITANT | ODIOUS |

Dr. Jekyll & Mr. Hyde Vocabulary

| MULTIFARIOUS | AUSTERE | PERPLEXITY | ENDOWED | LAMENTATION |
|---|---|---|---|---|
| INIQUITY | INCONGRUOUS | INVETERATELY | INCIPIENT | VOLATILE |
| CALAMITY | ACCOSTED | FREE SPACE | PERENNIAL | EFFICACY |
| ODIOUS | EXORBITANT | DISCONSOLATE | PECUNIARY | ABJECT |
| PROTEGE | CAPACIOUS | MIEN | CONFLAGRATION | REPROVE |

## Dr. Jekyll & Mr. Hyde Vocabulary

| | | | | |
|---|---|---|---|---|
| EFFICACY | AUSTERE | SOMBRE | INCIPIENT | INCOHERENCY |
| CALAMITY | ENIGMAS | UNOBTRUSIVE | CAPACIOUS | PERENNIAL |
| ABJECT | IMPERIOUS | FREE SPACE | INCONGRUOUS | GAUNT |
| VOLATILE | CONFLAGRATION | ENDOWED | LAMENTATION | DISINTERRED |
| INSENSATE | ACCOSTED | ODIOUS | INVETERATELY | EXORBITANT |

## Dr. Jekyll & Mr. Hyde Vocabulary

| | | | | |
|---|---|---|---|---|
| CONDONED | DETESTABLE | INIQUITY | REPOSE | MULTIFARIOUS |
| SEDULOUSLY | SCRUTINY | AVERSIONS | MIEN | PERPLEXITY |
| EMINENTLY | PROTEGE | FREE SPACE | REPROVE | DISCONSOLATE |
| EXORBITANT | INVETERATELY | ODIOUS | ACCOSTED | INSENSATE |
| DISINTERRED | LAMENTATION | ENDOWED | CONFLAGRATION | VOLATILE |

Dr. Jekyll & Mr. Hyde Vocabulary

| PERENNIAL | DETESTABLE | EFFICACY | PERPLEXITY | ABJECT |
|---|---|---|---|---|
| CAPACIOUS | SOMBRE | MIEN | ENIGMAS | GAUNT |
| REPROVE | UNOBTRUSIVE | FREE SPACE | INSENSATE | CONFLAGRATION |
| SEDULOUSLY | EMINENTLY | SCRUTINY | EXORBITANT | IMPERIOUS |
| LAMENTATION | REPOSE | RUMINATED | ODIOUS | INIQUITY |

Dr. Jekyll & Mr. Hyde Vocabulary

| AVERSIONS | AUSTERE | PECUNIARY | INCONGRUOUS | ACCOSTED |
|---|---|---|---|---|
| ENDOWED | INVETERATELY | VOLATILE | CALAMITY | PROTEGE |
| DISINTERRED | DISCONSOLATE | FREE SPACE | CONDONED | INCIPIENT |
| INIQUITY | ODIOUS | RUMINATED | REPOSE | LAMENTATION |
| IMPERIOUS | EXORBITANT | SCRUTINY | EMINENTLY | SEDULOUSLY |

www.ingramcontent.com/pod-product-compliance
Lightning Source LLC
Chambersburg PA
CBHW081456070526
44586CB00019B/2386